C000021194

CELTIC F.C.

- THE 25 YEAR RECORD

1970-71 to 1994-95 Seasons

SEASON BY SEASON WRITE-UPS
David Powter

EDITOR
Michael Robinson

CONTENTS

British Library Cataloguing in Publication Data

A catalogue record for this book is available from the British Library

ISBN 0-947808-58-2

Copyright © 1995; SOCCER BOOK PUBLISHING LTD. (01472-696226)

72, St. Peters' Avenue, Cleethorpes, Sth. Humberside, DN35 8HU, England

All rights are reserved. No part of this publication may be reproduced, stored into a retrieval system or transmitted, in any form or by any means, electronic, mechanical, photocopying, recording, or otherwise, without the prior written permission of Soccer Book Publishing Ltd.

Printed by Redwood Books, Kennet House, Kennet Way, Trowbridge, Wilts.

CELTIC F.C.
- Seasons 1970-71 to 1994-95

The 1994-95 campaign finished on a happy note for Celtic who collected their first trophy in 6 years by lifting the Scottish Cup. Twenty-five seasons ago, the club were enjoying the most successful period in their history. Fourteen trophies had already been secured in 7 seasons and another 21 were about to be won in the following 19 years.

Jock Stein's sixth full season as Celtic manager got off to a flier, with his side winning 11 of the first twelve. However, they were made to work hard for the 1970-71 title by Aberdeen, who were the only successful visitors to Parkhead. Nevertheless, Celtic regained their crown by collecting points from a backlog of fixtures and finished 2 points ahead.

A terrible tragedy marred the campaign when 66 spectators died (and over 200 were injured) in a crush during the closing seconds of Celtic's visit to Ibrox Park on 2nd January 1971.

Harry Hood's coolness from the penalty-spot clinched the Double as Rangers were beaten 2-1 in a Scottish Cup final replay. It was the Bhoys' revenge for an Old Firm League Cup final defeat in October.

Celtic netted 24 times as they brushed Kokkola and Waterford aside on their way to the European Cup quarter-final. However, they found the eventual competition winners Ajax too good for them in Amsterdam.

Stein's side went one stage further in the 1971-72 European Cup. Both semi-final ties with Internazionale ended goalless, but the Milan side triumphed 5-4 on penalties. Celtic netted 96 goals in their romp to their seventh successive title, 10 points ahead of Aberdeen. Sixteen of those goals came from 2 matches against Clyde, with Kenny Dalglish netting his first League goal in the opening day meeting. Dixie Deans was the top scorer (with 19) and he also scored in every round of the Scottish Cup, including a hat-trick in an emphatic 6-1 victory over Hibs in the final. Six months earlier, Celtic had been on the wrong end of an emphatic scoreline when Partick Thistle defeated them 4-1 in the League

Cup final.

With Parkhead under reconstruction, the first 2 home games of 1972-73 were played at Hampden Park. Nevertheless, both ended in comfortable 'home' victories including the crucial clash with Rangers. The Gers proved to be Celtic's main challengers and Stein's side had to win all of their last 7 matches to cling on to the title by a single point.

The Bhoys lost both domestic cup finals in 1972-73 as Rangers gained some compensation in the Scottish Cup, and Hibs beat them in the League Cup. There was also little success in the European Cup with Ujpest Dozsa baulking them at the second hurdle.

Celtic had a longer European Cup run the following season, reaching the semi-final; but were defeated by Atletico Madrid. However, the champagne did flow in 1973-74 as Jock Stein's side secured their ninth consecutive Championship. They led the table from the end of October to finish 4 points in front of Hibs. The Celts reached the finals of both domestic cup competitions, but had contrasting fortunes. They lost to Dundee in the League Cup, but triumphed 3-0 against Dundee United in the Scottish Cup.

The Celts reached both finals again in 1974-75, for the fifth consecutive season. And, for the third time in their history, both ended in victory. Deans hit another final hat-trick in the 6-3 defeat of Hibs in the League version; while Paul Wilson (2) and Pat McCluskey were on the score-sheet as Airdrieonians were overcome 3-1 in the Scottish Cup.

Hopes of a lengthy 1974-75 European Cup campaign lay in ruins in Athens where Olympiakos Pireaeus proved too strong in the first round.

Worse was to follow, as dreams of a tenth consecutive title faded when they lost 3-0 at Ibrox in January. It had been only Celtic's second reverse of the season (the first was also inflicted by Rangers), but it sparked off a dire spell of 8 defeats in 15 matches. Celtic slumped to finish third, 11 points behind the Gers.

The Scottish League was reformatted in 1975 with Celtic one of 10 clubs who were to play each other 4 times in the Premier Division. Celtic led the field into the final stretch, but blew up and won just one of their last seven. They had to be

satisfied with second, 6 points behind Rangers. The Bhoys failed to beat the Gers in all 4 League encounters and also lost to them in the League Cup final.

For the first time in 8 seasons, Celtic failed to reach the Scottish Cup final in 1975-76. Their exit was as swift as it was unexpected in a third round tie at Motherwell. Celtic's European Cup Winners' Cup run also drew a blank or rather was ended by one at the quarter-final stage. Blank was the name of Sachsenring Zwickau scorer in both legs as the East Germans triumphed 2-1 on aggregate.

With Jock Stein recuperating from injuries sustained in a car crash, Celtic were managed by his assistant Sean Fallon in 1975-76. It was the first time in 12 years that they failed to win a trophy.

Stein was back at the helm in 1976-77 and, after losing to an extra-time Aberdeen goal in their 13th consecutive League Cup final, the Celts made a bold challenge to regain some glory in the League. Early leaders Dundee United and Aberdeen were overtaken by the end of 1976, and the title was clinched long before Rangers' late run into second place. Ronnie Glavin was the top scorer with 19.

The victorious Celtic team display the Scottish Cup after beating Rangers 1-0 in the 1977 Final.

Celtic also triumphed in the Scottish Cup, beating Rangers by a single Andy Lynch penalty in an undistinguished final spoilt by a rain affected pitch. Even more undistinguished was Celtic's run in the UEFA Cup when Wisla proved to be an insurmountable first hurdle.

The winds of change blew the wrong way for Celtic in 1977-78. Jock Stein moved 'upstairs' to become General Manager, with his former skipper Billy McNeill becoming team manager. More significantly, after 7 full seasons and 204 League appearances (112 goals), the maestro Kenny Dalglish departed to find more fame and glory at Anfield. Several injuries, most significantly to Danny McGrain, made it difficult for McNeill's side to settle and they finished 5th, 19 points behind the Champions Rangers. Shuggie Edvaldsson was the top scorer with 10.

There was to be no joy in any of the cups; SW Innsbruck punctured their

**The fans' favourite Bobby Lennox.
Bobby's joint testimonial game
(with Jimmy Johnstone) saw
60,000 fans pack Parkhead.**

European Cup dreams in the second round. Then in the space of 12 days, in March, Celtic were defeated in both domestic cups. Kilmarnock beat them in a Scottish Cup fourth round replay and Rangers beat them in extra-time in the League Cup final. For the first time in 16 years, Celtic had failed to qualify for Europe.

After more than 13 years at Parkhead, Jock Stein departed to become Leeds' manager in the summer of 1978. However, after just 44 days he returned north of the border to become the Scotland manager.

Celtic headed the early 1978-79 tables, after winning 6 of the first seven. However, they only won one of the next 11 as Dundee United roared into a clear lead before bad weather decimated the programme in January and February. Celtic were fresher for their 2 month break and, with McGrain fit again, gradually made up ground from 8th spot. Even so, with Rangers also in contention, a title triumph looked unlikely, especially as they lost the Old Firm clash on the last scheduled day of the season. However, the Bhoys won their last 4 rearranged fixtures including a vital fourth and deciding clash with the Gers in the last match. The gap between the two Glasgow sides was 3 points with Dundee United a further point behind in third.

There was to be no cup joy in 1978-79. They exited the Scottish Cup at the quarter-final stage and for the first time in 15 years failed to reach the final of the League Cup. Substitute Jim Casey put the ball into his own net to give Rangers a 3-2 semi-final victory in extra-time.

It was Alex Ferguson's improving Dons who prised the title away from them in 1979-80. Celtic led most of the term, but were defeated 4 times in the space of 18 days in April. Crucially, two were at the hands of Aberdeen who went on to edge the title from the Celts by just one point.

Aberdeen also had the Indian sign over McNeill's side in the Bell's League Cup quarter-final meeting at Parkhead. At the same stage of the European Cup, Celtic took a 2-0 lead into the second leg against Real Madrid. However, the Spaniards won 3-0 in front of a 110,000 Bernabeu crowd. The start of the new decade did not bring total cup misery though, as George McCluskey's extra-time goal proved enough to give Celtic a Scottish Cup final victory over

Rangers.

Despite taking just 2 draws from 4 meetings with their main rivals Aberdeen, Celtic took control of the Premier Division race by winning 13 out of the first 14 fixtures of 1981. Frank McGarvey top scored with 23, as the Bhoys finished a comfortable 7 points clear.

Dundee United scuppered Celtic's domestic cup hopes in 1980-81, winning at the semi-final stage in both competitions; while, Romanian surprise packets Poli Timisoara halted their progress in the European Cup Winners' Cup first round.

The Dons were once again their main title challengers in 1981-82, but Celtic led all the way to retain their crown by 2 points. The Celts failed to reach the quarter-finals of either domestic cup and fared no better in the European Cup where they exited to Juventus, 2-1 on aggregate.

Celtic finished one place in front of Aberdeen again in 1982-83; but had to settle for the runners-up berth as Dundee United won their last 6 games to be Champions by a single point.

Charlie Nicholas and Murdo McLeod netted the goals which gave Celtic a 2-1 League Cup final victory over Rangers. There was less joy in the other cups, Aberdeen beating them in a Scottish Cup semi-final; after disposing of Ajax, Celtic then found Real Sociedad too hot for them in the European Cup.

Billy McNeill left Parkhead at the end of June 1983 for a lucrative contract at Manchester City. His successor was David Hay, another former Celtic hero.

Hay's side got off to a flying start to 1983-84 by winning their first 5 games, but could not keep pace with Aberdeen, who took the title by 7 points. Brian McClair was the top scorer with 23, as his side finished second. The Bhoys also had to be content with runners-up medals in the two domestic cup competitions. Aberdeen got the better of them in the Scottish Cup final; but the turning point was Roy Aitken's dismissal (the first in a Scottish Cup final since 1929). The 10 men tired in extra-time and went down 2-1. Extra-time was also required in the League Cup final and on this occasion Rangers edged matters 3-2.

In the UEFA Cup, Celtic went out to Nottingham Forest in the third round. The

Bhoys were favourites after a 0-0 south of the border; but the English side raised their game and took the return 2-1.

It was a case of deja vu in the League in 1984-85. Celtic finished second to Aberdeen, the gap again being 7 points with McClair top scoring, this time with 19.

Dundee United knocked the Celts out of the Skol Cup in a quarter-final replay; but Hay's side took sweet revenge in the Scottish Cup final 2 months later. Davie Provan and McGarvey were the scorers as their side came from behind to win 2-1.

Celtic made an extraordinary exit from the European Cup Winners' Cup in the second round. After trailing Rapid Vienna 3-1 from the first leg, the Bhoys netted 3 times to pull off a splendid 4-3 aggregate victory. However, UEFA subsequently annulled the game because of the bad behaviour of a minority of the Parkhead fans. The 'replay' had to be more than 100 miles from Glasgow and went ahead at Old Trafford 5 weeks later. Celtic could not raise their game again and the Austrians won 1-0.

Jock Stein's death after Scotland's victory in Cardiff in September 1985 cast a shadow over the start of the 1985-86 campaign. His old club responded by lifting the title in his memory. However, they needed to win all their last 8 games to do so. Even then, the Bhoys were lucky as Hearts led by 2 points and a superior goal difference on the last day of the season. Needing only a point to be sure, the Edinburgh side went down 2-0 at Dundee, while Celtic leap-frogged them with a 5-0 victory at St Mirren.

Hibs put paid to all Celtic's domestic cup hopes in 1985-86, by beating them in two high-scoring quarter-finals at Easter Road. Celtic lost on penalties in the Skol Cup after a 4-4 draw; and then went down by the odd goal in 7 in the Scottish Cup. There was no success in the European Cup Winners' Cup either, despite holding Atletico Madrid 1-1 away in the first round. The Bhoys' challenge crumbled on their home soil as the Spaniards won 2-1 behind 'closed doors', another consequence of the Rapid Vienna game a season earlier.

1986-87 was Brian McClair's last season at Parkhead before he moved to Old Trafford. He finished off as top scorer with 35, to bring his tally to 99 from just

145 League games. Celtic had an unassailable looking lead at the halfway point, but had to settle for second after their stumble allowed Rangers to stride past them and finish 6 points clear.

Celtic also came second to their Glasgow rivals in the Skol Cup final; and their European Cup Winners' Cup campaign ground to a halt at the second hurdle. Dynamo Kiev held the upper hand throughout the 180 minutes and the Bhoys were defeated 4-1 on aggregate.

Hay was replaced by the club's former boss Billy McNeill during the close season and his return signalled a brief restoration of fortunes. Led superbly on the field by the determined Roy Aitken, the Celts swept to the top of the table in November and pulled away to clinch their 35th League title by 10 points from Hearts. Celtic's Centenary year was in fact garnished by the Double, as they came from behind to defeat Dundee United 2-1 in the Scottish Cup final. Frank McAvennie netted both goals in the last 15 minutes, the winner coming on the stroke of time.

Earlier in 1987-88, Celtic had lost narrowly in both the Skol Cup (quarter-final) and the UEFA Cup (first round). Aberdeen triumphed 1-0 in the former; while Borussia Dortmund were their conquerors in Europe. Celtic took a 2-1 lead to Dortmund, but the Germans went through by the minimum 2-0 margin.

Celtic were also defeated by German opposition in the following term, Werder Bremen proving too strong in the European Cup. There was little joy in the the Skol Cup either as they exited at the quarter-final stage. Nevertheless Roy Aitken did hold one cup aloft in 1988-89, as a Joe Miller special won the Old Firm Scottish Cup final.

However, it was the blue half of Glasgow which celebrated League glory, with Celtic finishing third, 10 points adrift. The Parkhead fans had become resigned to losing their grip on the title after their side lost 5 of the first 8 games. What those fans were not to know was just how long Rangers would keep the trophy!

McNeill's men got off to a better start in 1989-90 and led the table at the end of November, but their failure to score in 14 of their last 26 fixtures ground them almost to a halt. After winning just twice in the second half of the season they finished 5th, 17 points behind Rangers. Dariusz Dziekanowski was the top

scorer with 8 out of a paltry total of 37.

Celtic exited the European Cup Winners' Cup at the first hurdle on away goals, despite Dziekanowski's 4 goals in his side's 5-4 'victory' over Partizan in the second leg at Parkhead. Any hopes of domestic glory were ended by Aberdeen. A single goal was enough to scupper them in the last four of the Skol Cup, while the Dons won the Scottish Cup final on penalties after a scoreless 120 minutes. The Celts lost the shoot-out on the 20th kick by 9-8!

A sluggish start in 1990-91 was followed by a mediocre middle, and it took a late rally of 11 victories from the final 15 fixtures to edge McNeill's men into third, 14 points behind Rangers.

Eventual winners Motherwell defeated the Celts in a Scottish Cup semi-final replay. The green and white hoops had gone one better in the Skol Cup, but were beaten by Rangers 2-1 in extra-time.

For the first time in 27 years, Celtic had gone two seasons without collecting any silverware. Billy McNeill paid the price and collected his P45. The Celtic Board gambled on the highly respected but untried Liam Brady as his replacement.

Brady's side got off to a good start in 1991-92; however, Aberdeen and Rangers soon got the better of them and they lost confidence. Despite winning 10 on the trot in the second half of the campaign, Celtic failed to compete with the Gers and finished 10 points adrift in third (just qualifying for Europe on goal difference). Rangers got the better of them again in the last four of the Scottish Cup, while their inability with spot-kicks cost them in a Skol Cup quarter-final shoot-out with Airdrieonians.

Celtic's return to Europe was ended by Neuchatel Xamax in the third round of the UEFA Cup. They won the second leg 1-0, but the damage had already been done by a crushing 5-1 defeat in Switzerland.

The Celts never got on terms with Rangers in 1992-93 and finished 13 points behind in third. There was also little satisfaction from their cup runs. Falkirk and Borussia Dortmund knocked them out at the second hurdle of the Scottish and UEFA cups, respectively; and Aberdeen were too good for them in a Skol

Cup semi-final.

Liam Brady resigned on 7th October 1993, after his side had picked up just 2 wins from the opening 10 games. The following day his assistant Joe Jordan declined to take over on a caretaker basis; so, later that month, former Celtic striker Lou Macari returned to take the reins.

Macari lifted the Bhoys into a five horse Championship race and if they had won all 4 final games rather than drawing them they would have reclaimed the crown. Instead they finished 4th, 4 points adrift of Rangers.

The Gers had earlier held the upper-hand in the Skol Cup, disposing of Brady's Celtic in the semi-final. Macari had no cup luck in 1993-94: he inherited a 1-0 lead over Sporting Lisbon in the second round of the UEFA Cup, but his side lost 2-0 in Portugal. His side's Scottish Cup run also lasted just one game, at Motherwell.

The Celtic Board and Lou Macari were often at odds on various key issues and after just 8 months in the job the manager was given the sack on 16th June 1994.

Much to the Celtic faithful's approval, Macari's successor was another of their

'Paradise' - Celtic Park before redevelopment

former stars, the Kilmarnock boss Tommy Burns. After 5 blank years, Burns' immediate aim was to bring a trophy back to Parkhead. It looked as if it might happen early in 1994-95 when they met Raith Rovers in the Coca-Cola Cup final. However, after the scores ended 2-2, a shoot-out came into operation. Typically, Celtic lost their nerve first and it was their First Division opponents who lifted the trophy by 6-5 on penalties.

The Bhoys played all their 1994-95 home games at Hampden Park, while Celtic Park was being redeveloped. They made no impression in the League, finishing 4th, 18 points behind Rangers, Champions for the 7th season in succession.

However, there was still a last chance of glory with a Scottish Cup final against another First Division side, Airdrieonians. This time there was no slip up, as Peter Van Hooijdonk's early goal proved enough to secure the Celts a 30th Scottish Cup. It was their 22nd trophy in 25 seasons and gave their fans renewed optimism about their team's prospects.

1970-71

1	Aug	29	(h)	Morton	W	2-0	Lennox 2	35,000
2	Sep	5	(a)	Clyde	W	5-0	Macari 2, Hay, Davidson, McHugh (og)	22,000
3		12	(h)	Rangers	W	2-0	Hughes, Murdoch	73,000
4		19	(a)	Hibernian	L	0-2		36,423
5		26	(h)	Dundee	W	3-0	Johnstone 2, Macari	30,000
6	Oct	3	(a)	Dunfermline A	W	2-0	Macari, Wallace (pen)	15,000
7		10	(h)	St. Johnstone	W	1-0	Wallace	37,000
8		17	(a)	Airdrieonians	W	3-1	Hood 2, Lennox	20,000
9		28	(h)	Heart of Midlothian	W	3-2	Wallace 2, Hood	18,000
10		31	(a)	Motherwell	W	5-0	Hood 3 (1 pen), Connelly, Johnstone	20,000
11	Nov	7	(h)	Cowdenbeath	W	3-0	Connelly 2, Wallace	19,572
12		14	(h)	Kilmarnock	W	3-0	Murdoch, Wallace, Johnstone	27,000
13		21	(a)	Falkirk	D	0-0		18,700
14		28	(h)	St. Mirren	W	3-0	Davidson 2, Gemmell	25,000
15	Dec	5	(a)	Dundee U	W	2-1	Davidson, Markland (og)	18,000
16		12	(h)	Aberdeen	L	0-1		63,000
17		19	(a)	Ayr U	W	2-1	Hughes, Hood	15,000
18		26	(a)	Morton	W	3-0	Chalmers, Lennox, Wallace	18,000
19	Jan	2	(a)	Rangers	D	1-1	Johnstone	80,000
20		9	(h)	Hibernian	W	2-1	Callaghan, Hood	35,000
21		16	(a)	Dundee	W	8-1	Hood 2, Wallace 2, Johnstone 2, Houston (og), Callaghan	20,000
22		30	(h)	Dunfermline A	W	1-0	Wallace	25,000
23	Feb	6	(a)	St. Johnstone	L	2-3	Wallace, Hood	19,000
24		20	(h)	Airdrieonians	W	4-1	Wallace 2, Hood, Macari	27,000
25		27	(a)	Heart of Midlothian	D	1-1	Hood	24,000
26	Mar	13	(a)	Cowdenbeath	W	5-1	Hood 2 (1 pen), Hughes, McNeill, Lennox	8,500
27		20	(a)	Kilmarnock	W	4-1	Hood 2, Hughes, Davidson	16,000
28		27	(h)	Falkirk	W	4-0	Hood 2, Hughes, Wallace	22,000
29	Apr	10	(h)	Dundee U	D	1-1	Wallace	30,000
30		12	(h)	Motherwell	W	3-0	Wallace, Johnstone, Hood	23,000
31		17	(a)	Aberdeen	D	1-1	Hood	35,000
32		27	(a)	St. Mirren	D	2-2	Hood, Lennox	20,000
33		29	(h)	Ayr U	W	2-0	Lennox, Wallace	25,000
34	May	1	(h)	Clyde	W	6-1	Lennox 3, Wallace 2, Chalmers	35,000

FINAL LEAGUE POSITION : 1st in Division One

Appearances

Sub. Appearances

Goals

Williams	McGrair	Gemmell	Murdoch	McNeill	Brogan J	Johnstone	Hay	Hood	Lennox	Macari	Connelly	Hughes	Davidson	Callaghan	Wilson	Wallace	Quinn	Craig	Cattenach	Dalglish	Fallon	Chalmers	Auld	Clark	
1	2	3*	4	5	6	7	8	9	10	11	12														1
1	2		4*	5	6		3	9	10	11	8	7	12												2
1	2		4	5	6	7	3	9	10		8	11													3
1	2		4	5	6	7	3	9	10		8	11													4
1	2		4		6	7	3	9	12	10	5			8	11*										5
1	2		4	5		8	3	12	11	10	6		7*			9									6
1		3		5		7	2	9	10	11	4			6*		8	12								7
1			4	5		7*	3	10	11		8					9	2	6		12					8
1			4	5		7	3	8	11		10					9	2	6							9
1			4	5		7	3	8*	11	12	10					9	2	6							10
1			4	5		7	3	8	10		11					9	2	6							11
1		3	4*	5	6	7	12	8	10		11					9	2								12
1		3	4	5	6	7	10	11*	8	9						12	2								13
		3	4	5	6		10	8*	12	11	7					9	2				1				14
		3	4	5	6	7	9	8	11		10						2				1				15
		3	4	5	6	7	10	12	9		8*	11					2				1				16
1		3	4	5	7	6	9	8	12		11*	10					2								17
1		3	4		6		8	11			5	10				9	2						7		18
1		3	4		7	6	8	11			5	10				9	2								19
1		3	4	5	6	7	9	11	10		8						2								20
1		3	4	5	6	7	9	10			8						2					11			21
1		3	4*	5	6	7	12	9	10		8						2					11			22
1		3	5	4	7	6	9	11*	10		8						2					12			23
1		3		5	6	7	2	8	11	12	4*	10				9									24
1		3		5	6	7	2	8	11		4	10				9									25
1		3		5	6		8	12	11	10	4					9*	2						7		26
1		3		5	6	7	2	8*	11	10	4					9						12			27
1		3	12	5	6*	7	2	8	11	10	4					9									28
1		3		5	6	7	2	8			4					9				10		11			29
1		3	12	5	6	7	8	11*	10		4					9	2								30
1		3		5	6	7	8	11*	10		4					9	2		12						31
1		3		5	6	7	8	11	10		4					9	2								32
1		3		5	6	7	8	11	10		4					9*	2			12					33
1		3	4	5		7		11								8	2					9	10	6	34
31	7	19	21	31	26	30	27	27	22	8	22	14	6	19	1	25	22	4	1	3	3	3	4	1	
			2			1	3	2	3	2			1			1	2	2		1	1				
		1	2	1		8	1	22	10	5	3	5		5	2	19	2								

1971-72

1	Sep	4	(h)	Clyde	W	9-1	Lennox 3, Macari 2, McNeill, Callaghan, Murdoch, Dalglish	30,000
2		11	(a)	Rangers	W	3-2	Macari, Dalglish, Johnstone	69,000
3		18	(h)	Morton	W	3-1	Hood, Lennox, Clark (og)	35,000
4		25	(a)	Airdrieonians	W	5-0	Macari 3, Lennox, Dalglish	20,000
5	Oct	2	(h)	St. Johnstone	L	0-1		38,000
6		9	(a)	Hibernian	W	1-0	Macari	40,671
7		16	(h)	Dundee	W	3-1	Dalglish 3	32,000
8		27	(a)	Dunfermline A	W	2-1	McNeill, Lennox	16,000
9		30	(a)	Ayr U	W	1-0	Dalglish	18,000
10	Nov	6	(h)	Aberdeen	D	1-1	Hood	64,000
11		13	(a)	Dundee U	W	5-1	Hood 2, Macari, Lennox, Dalglish	18,500
12		20	(h)	Falkirk	W	2-0	Dalglish, McNeill	25,000
13		27	(a)	Partick Thistle	W	5-1	Dalglish, Hood, Johnstone, Deans, Strachan (og)	33,000
14	Dec	4	(h)	Kilmarnock	W	5-1	Dalglish 2, Johnstone 2, Deans	28,000
15		11	(h)	East Fife	W	2-1	Deans 2	20,000
16		18	(a)	Motherwell	W	5-1	Dalglish 2, Johnstone, Deans, Lennox	19,000
17		25	(h)	Heart of Midlothian	W	3-2	Hood, Johnstone, Deans	34,000
18	Jan	1	(a)	Clyde	W	7-0	Hood 2, Deans 2, Dalglish, Davidson, Mulheron (og)	20,000
19		3	(h)	Rangers	W	2-1	Johnstone, Brogan J	77,811
20		8	(a)	Morton	D	1-1	Hood	18,000
21		15	(h)	Airdrieonians	W	2-0	Dalglish, Lennox	27,000
22		22	(a)	St. Johnstone	W	3-0	Deans 2, Dalglish	14,300
23		29	(h)	Hibernian	W	2-1	Deans, Hood	38,500
24	Feb	19	(h)	Dunfermline A	W	1-0	Macari	25,000
25	Mar	4	(h)	Ayr U	W	2-0	Deans 2	23,000
26		11	(a)	Aberdeen	D	1-1	Lennox	33,000
27		25	(a)	Falkirk	W	1-0	Davidson	16,000
28	Apr	1	(h)	Partick Thistle	W	3-1	Davidson 2, Johnstone	29,000
29		8	(a)	Kilmarnock	W	3-1	Davidson, Deans, Wilson	14,000
30		15	(a)	East Fife	W	3-0	Deans 2, Hood	12,086
31		22	(h)	Motherwell	W	5-2	Deans 2, Murdoch 2 (2 pens), Lennox	20,000
32		25	(h)	Dundee U	W	3-0	Deans, Johnstone, Lennox	13,000
33		29	(a)	Heart of Midlothian	L	1-4	Murdoch (pen)	15,500
34	May	1	(a)	Dundee	D	1-1	Macari	10,500

FINAL LEAGUE POSITION : 1st in Division One

Appearances

Sub. Appearances

Goals

Williams	Hay	Gemmell	Murdoch	McNeill	Connelly	Johnstone	Lennox	Dalglish	Callaghan	Macari	Wallace	Brogan J	Hood	Craig	Hughes	Connaghan	Davidson	Quinn	Deans	Wilson	McGrain	McClusky P	#
1	2	3	4	5	6	7	8	9*	10	11	12												1
1	2		4	5	6	7	8	9	10	11		3											2
1	2		4	5	6		8	9*	10	11	12	3	7										3
1	4			5	6		8	9	10	11	7	3		2*	12								4
1	4			5	6	7	12	8	10	11	9	3*		2									5
1	2	3	4	5	6	7	8		11	10			9										6
1	2	3	4	5	6	7		8	10	11			9										7
	3		4*	5	6		10	7	11	8		12	9	2		1							8
	4			5	6		10	7		8		3	11	2		1	9						9
	4			5	6	7		9	11	10		3	8	2		1							10
	4			5	6	7	12	9*	11	10		3	8	2		1							11
	6			5		7	10	9	4	8			11	2		1		3					12
	2			5	6	7		8	4	10			11			1		3	9				13
	2			5	6	7		8	4	10*			11			1		3	9	12			14
	2			5		7		8	4			6	10			1		3	9	11			15
	2			5	6	7	8	4	10				11			1		3	9				16
	2			5	6	7	8	4	10				11			1		3	9				17
	2			5	6		8	4	10			3	11			1	7		9*	12			18
	2			5	6	7	8	4	10			3	11			1			9				19
	2			5	6	7	8	4	10			3	11			1			9				20
	2			5	6	7	10	8	4			3	11			1			9				21
1	4			5	6	7	10	8	12			3	11*	2					9				22
1	4			5	6	7	10	8				3	11	2					9				23
1	2		4	5	6		10	7		8		3	11						9				24
1	2		4	5	6		11	8*	10			3	7						9			12	25
1	8		4	5	6		11	9*	12	10		3	7								2		26
1	4			5	6		8	10	12								7	3	9	11	2*		27
1			4	5	6	7	11		10				2				8	3	9				28
1			4	5	6	7	11*		10				2				8		9	12	3		29
1			4	5	6		8	10	11*			7	2					3	9		12		30
1			4	5	6	7	11	8	10				2						9		3		31
1			4	5	6	7	11	8	10			3	.2						9				32
1	8		4	5	6			11		10		3	7	2					9				33
1				5	6	7	11	4	10	9		3		2					8				34
20	28	3	15	34	32	23	24	31	28	19	2	20	24	16		14	5	9	21	2	2	2	
							2		2	1	2	1			1				2	1	2		
		4	3		9	12	17	1	10		1	11						5	19	1			

1972-73

1	Sep	2	(h)	Kilmarnock	W	6-2	Hood 3, Deans 2, Murdoch (pen)	11,651
2		9	(a)	Morton	W	2-0	Murdoch 2 (1 pen)	15,000
3		16	(h)	Rangers	W	3-1	Dalglish, Johnstone, Macari	50,416
4		23	(a)	Dundee	L	0-2		18,300
5		30	(h)	Ayr U	W	1-0	Deans	25,000
6	Oct	7	(h)	Airdrieonians	D	1-1	Lennox	22,000
7		14	(a)	Partick Thistle	W	4-0	Lennox, Hay, Deans, Dalglish	25,699
8		21	(h)	East Fife	W	3-0	Lennox, Hood, Deans	20,000
9		28	(a)	Aberdeen	W	3-2	Deans, Macari, Dalglish	36,000
10	Nov	4	(h)	Dundee U	W	3-1	Johnstone, Macari, Dalglish	32,000
11		11	(a)	Motherwell	W	5-0	Dalglish 2, Hood 2, McCallum (og)	12,439
12		18	(h)	Heart of Midlothian	W	4-2	Dalglish, Deans, Johnstone, Hood	28,000
13		25	(a)	Falkirk	W	3-2	Dalglish 2, Deans	15,000
14	Dec	2	(a)	Dumbarton	W	6-1	McCluskey P 3, Johnstone, Cushley (og), Hood	15,000
15		16	(a)	Arbroath	W	2-1	Hood 2	5,481
16		23	(h)	Hibernian	D	1-1	Dalglish	45,000
17	Jan	6	(a)	Rangers	L	1-2	Smith (og)	67,000
18		13	(h)	Dundee	W	2-1	Dalglish, Johnstone	27,000
19		20	(a)	Ayr U	W	3-1	Dalglish 2, Deans	11,500
20		27	(a)	Airdrieonians	L	1-2	Deans	18,000
21	Feb	7	(a)	Kilmarnock	W	4-0	Dalglish 2, Johnstone, Callaghan	11,000
22		10	(h)	Partick Thistle	D	1-1	Murdoch	32,000
23		17	(a)	East Fife	D	2-2	Deans 2	11,557
24		28	(h)	St. Johnstone	W	4-0	Lennox 2, Hay, Dalglish	19,000
25	Mar	3	(h)	Aberdeen	W	2-0	Lennox (pen), Dalglish	38,000
26		6	(h)	Morton	W	1-0	Wilson	23,000
27		10	(a)	Dundee U	D	2-2	Lennox 2	18,000
28		24	(a)	Heart of Midlothian	W	2-0	Lennox, Deans	22,000
29		31	(h)	Falkirk	W	4-0	Lennox 2 (1 pen), Deans, Hood	19,000
30	Apr	3	(h)	Motherwell	W	2-0	Dalglish, Deans	22,000
31		14	(a)	St. Johnstone	W	3-1	Dalglish 2, Johnstone	14,500
32		18	(a)	Dumbarton	W	5-0	Deans 3, Dalglish, Callaghan	27,000
33		21	(h)	Arbroath	W	4-0	Deans, Hood, Hay, Winchester (og)	28,000
34		28	(a)	Hibernian	W	3-0	Deans 2, Dalglish	45,453

FINAL LEAGUE POSITION : 1st in Division One

Appearances

Sub. Appearances

Goals

	Connaghan	McGrain	Brogan J	Murdoch	McNeill	Connelly	Hood	Dalglish	Deans	Callaghan	Wilson	Lennox	Williams	McCluskey P	Macari	Johnstone	Quinn	Davidson	Hay	Hunter	Lynch	McLaughlin	
1	1	2	3*	4	5	6	7	8	9	10	11	12											1
2		2		4	5	6	7	8	9	10*		11	1	3	12								2
3		2		4	5	6	12	8	9	11			1	3	10	7*							3
4		2		4	5	6		9	12	11			1	8*	10	7	3						4
5		2		4	5		11	8	9	6			1	3	10	7							5
6	1	2		4	5	6	7*	8		10		11		3		9		12					6
7			3*	4	5	6	12	7	9	10		11	1		8				2				7
8		2		4*	5	6	12	7	9	10		11	1		8				3				8
9		2			5	6	7		9	10		11	1	3	8				4				9
10			3		5	4	12	8	9*			11	1	6	10	7			2				10
11		2	3		5		10	9	8	11			1	4		7			6				11
12		2				6	10	9	8	11		12	1	4		7	3*		5				12
13	1	2	3		5		7	8	9	11*		12		4	10				6				13
14	1	2	3	10	5		7		9	8*		12		4		11			6				14
15		2	3	10	5		8	11	9			12	1	4*		7			6				15
16			3		5	6	11	8	9	10		12	1	4		7*			2				16
17			3		5	6	12	8	9	10			1	4*	11	7			2				17
18		2	3	4	5	6	11	8	9*	10		12	1			7							18
19		2	3	4	5	6	11	8*	9	10		12	1			7							19
20		2	3	4	5	6	11	8*	9	10		12				7				1			20
21		2		4	5	6	12	8	9*	10		11				7	3			1			21
22		2		4	5	6		8	9	10		11*				7	3			1	12		22
23		2		4	5	6	10	8	9			11				7	3			1			23
24		2		4	5	6		8	9			11				7*	3		10	1	12		24
25		2		4*	5	6	10	8	9			11			12	7	3			1			25
26		2			5	6	10	7	9		8	11					3		4	1			26
27		2			5	6	10*	8	9		12	11				7	3		4	1			27
28		2	3	4	5	6	7*		9	12		11						8	10	1			28
29		2	3	4	5	6	7*		9	11		8							10	1	12		29
30		2	3		5	6	7	8	9	11		10							4	1			30
31		2	3	4	5	6		8	9	11						7			10	1			31
32		2	3	4	5	6	12	8	9	11						7*			10	1			32
33		2	3	4	5	6	7	8	9	11*		12							10	1			33
34		2	3	4	5	6		8	9	11						7			10	1			34
	4	30	20	24	30	32	22	32	30	27	2	15	15	14	10	21	9	1	21	15			
							7		1	2		8		1	1	1	1	1	1		1	2	
				4			12	22	21	2	1	11		3	3	7			3				

19

1973-74

1	Sep	1	(a)	Dunfermline A	W	3-2	Hood, Wilson, Leishman (og)	14,705
2		8	(h)	Clyde *	W	5-0	Lennox 3 (1 pen), Dalglish, McGrain	27,000
3		15	(a)	Rangers	W	1-0	Johnstone	60,000
4		29	(a)	St. Johnstone	L	1-2	Deans	12,000
5	Oct	6	(h)	Motherwell	W	2-0	Deans, Wilson	32,000
6		13	(a)	Dundee	W	1-0	Callaghan	17,433
7		20	(h)	Hibernian	D	1-1	McCluskey P	34,000
8		27	(a)	Heart of Midlothian	W	3-1	Dalglish 2, Connelly	33,000
9	Nov	3	(h)	East Fife	W	4-2	Deans 2, Dalglish, Hood	23,000
10		10	(a)	Ayr U	W	1-0	Dalglish	15,000
11		17	(h)	Partick Thistle †	W	7-0	Deans 6, Lennox	22,000
12		24	(a)	Dumbarton	W	2-0	Dalglish, Lennox (pen)	9,000
13	Dec	1	(a)	Arbroath	W	2-1	Dalglish, Wilson	5,708
14		8	(h)	Dundee U	D	3-3	Dalglish, Hood, Callaghan	19,000
15		22	(h)	Falkirk	W	6-0	Deans 4, Dalglish, Lennox	11,000
16		29	(h)	Dunfermline A	W	6-0	Deans 2, Dalglish 2, Hood 2	21,000
17	Jan	1	(a)	Clyde	W	2-0	Dalglish, Lennox	10,630
18		5	(h)	Rangers	W	1-0	Lennox	55,000
19		19	(h)	St. Johnstone	W	3-0	Murray, Lennox (pen), Argue (og)	19,000
20	Feb	2	(a)	Motherwell	L	2-3	Murray, Lennox	16,669
21		10	(h)	Dundee ‡	L	1-2	Hay	40,000
22		23	(a)	Hibernian	W	4-2	Deans 2, Dalglish, Wilson	48,544
23	Mar	2	(h)	Heart of Midlothian	W	1-0	Deans	32,000
24		16	(h)	Ayr U	W	4-0	Deans 2, Johnstone 2 (2 pens)	26,000
25		23	(a)	Partick Thistle	L	0-2		20,000
26		30	(h)	Dumbarton	D	3-3	Deans, Dalglish, Wilson	19,000
27	Apr	6	(h)	Arbroath	W	1-0	Dalglish	22,000
28		13	(a)	Dundee U	W	2-0	Murray, Hay	17,000
29		17	(a)	East Fife	W	6-1	Dalglish 2, Hood 2, Lennox, Deans	6,970
30		20	(h)	Aberdeen	W	2-0	Deans, Lennox	31,000
31		27	(a)	Falkirk	D	1-1	Dalglish	13,500
32		29	(a)	Aberdeen	D	0-0		10,500
33		30	(h)	Morton	D	1-1	McLaughlin	9,000
34	May	6	(a)	Morton	D	0-0		6,500

FINAL LEAGUE POSITION : 1st in Division One

Appearances

Sub. Appearance

Goals

* Everyone in the team wore number-eight shorts to celebrate Celtic's eighth League Championship title in succession.
† Deans' six goals created a post-war club record for a competitive match.
‡ Celtic's first League match on a Sunday.

Hunter	McGrain	Brogan J	Murray	McNeill	Connelly	McLaughlin	Hood	Dalglish	Hay	Lennox	Wilson	Johnstone	Callaghan	Deans	McCluskey P	MacDonald	Lynch	Quinn	McNamara	Ritchie	Davidson	Bone	Cannaghan	Welsh	
1	2	3	4	5	6	7*	8	9	10	11	12														1
1	2	3	4	5	6	7*	8†	9	10	11	13	12													2
1	2	3	4	5	6		8*	9	10		11	7	12												3
1	2	3	4	5	6		11*	8	10			7	12	9											4
1	2	3	4	5	6		8				11	7	10	9											5
1	2	3	4	5	6		7	9	10		12		11	8*											6
1	2	3	4	5†	6	7*	8	10	9				11	12	13										7
1	2	3	8		6		11	10			7			9	4	5									8
1	2	3*	8	5	6		10	11†			7			12	9	4	13								9
1	2	3	8	5	6		11				7		10	9	4										10
1	2		6	5			8	11†		7*	13		10	9	4			3	12						11
1	2	3	6	5			8	11		7*	9	12	10		4										12
1	2	3	6	5			8	11			9	7	10		4										13
1	2	3	6	5			7*	11	8	12	9		10		4										14
1	2	3	8	5			7	10	6	11				9	4										15
1	2	3	8	5*			7	10	6	11†	13			9	4					12					16
1	2	3	8	5			7	10	6	11				9	4										17
1	2	3	8	5			7	10	6	11				9	4										18
1	2	3	8	5			7	10	6	11*					4		12	9							19
1	2	3	8	5			7	10	6	11				9	4										20
1	2	3	8	5	4		7*	10	6	11			12	9											21
1	2	3	8	5	4		7	10	6	11				9											22
1	2*	3	8		4		7	10	6	11				9†	12	5				13					23
	3	4	5	6			13	11†	2	12		7	10	9							8*	1			24
	3	4	5				13	11	2	12		7*	10	9	6						8†	1			25
1	2	3	4	5			8	12		11		7	10*	9	6										26
	2		4	5			8*	11	3	12		7	10	9	6							1			27
	2	3	4	5			7*	9	10	11			12		6						8	1			28
	2		4	5			7	8*		11		12	10	9	6				3			1			29
	2	3	8	5			10	11	4	13		7*	12	9†	6							1			30
	12	3	4*	5			7	8	2	11			10	9	6							1			31
1	2		6				12	7	8	11				9*	4		3			10				5	32
1				5		12	4		10	8	7			`9	3		11*	2			6				33
	3		8				10	13	2	11		7*	6	12	4					9†		1	5		34
26	29	30	32	30	14	2	28	31	25	17	10	13	16	24	23	2	1	3	1	3	3	8	3		
	1				1	3	2		2	9	2	6	2	2		2		1	1		1				
	1		3		1	1	7	18	2	12	5	3	2	24	1										

1974-75

1	Aug	3	(h)	Kilmarnock	W	5-0	Johnstone, Wilson, Murray (pen), Davidson, Dalglish	27,000
2	Sep	7	(a)	Clyde	W	4-2	Davidson, McCluskey P, Dalglish, Lennox	15,000
3		14	(h)	Rangers	L	1-2	Dalglish	60,000
4		21	(a)	Motherwell	W	2-1	Lennox 2 (2 pens)	13,113
5		28	(h)	Ayr U	W	5-3	Wilson 2, Deans, Dalglish, Hood	20,000
6	Oct	5	(a)	Dumbarton	W	3-1	Johnstone, Deans, Dalglish	13,000
7		12	(h)	Arbroath	W	1-0	Murray	16,000
8		19	(h)	Hibernian	W	5-0	Deans 3, Johnstone, Murray (pen)	39,000
9	Nov	2	(h)	Aberdeen	W	1-0	Wilson	29,000
10		6	(a)	Partick Thistle	W	2-1	Deans, Dalglish	15,500
11		9	(a)	Dundee U	D	0-0		15,300
12		16	(h)	Airdieonians	W	6-0	Murray 2, McNeill, Glavin, Wilson, Lennox (pen)	26,000
13		23	(a)	Heart of Midlothian	D	1-1	Wilson	23,000
14		30	(a)	Morton	W	1-0	Murray	17,000
15	Dec	7	(h)	Dunfermline A	W	2-1	Bone, Hood	20,000
16		14	(a)	Dundee	W	6-0	Dalglish 3, Johnstone 2, Wilson	14,901
17		21	(h)	St. Johnstone	W	3-1	Dalglish, Murray, McCluskey P (pen)	20,000
18		28	(a)	Kilmarnock	W	1-0	Dalglish	17,500
19	Jan	1	(h)	Clyde	W	5-1	Callaghan 2, Deans, Dalglish, Glavin	20,000
20		4	(a)	Rangers	L	0-3		70,000
21		11	(h)	Motherwell	L	2-3	Hood 2	26,000
22		18	(a)	Ayr U	W	5-1	Deans 2, Murray, Hood, McDonald (og)	14,500
23	Feb	8	(a)	Arbroath	D	2-2	Hood, Dalglish	7,500
24		11	(h)	Dumbarton	D	2-2	Hood, Wilson	15,000
25		22	(a)	Hibernian	L	1-2	Wilson	29,354
26	Mar	1	(h)	Partick Thistle	W	3-2	Hood, Dalglish, McCluskey P (pen)	21,000
27		12	(a)	Aberdeen	L	2-3	Lynch 2	16,000
28		15	(h)	Dundee U	L	0-1		20,000
29		22	(a)	Airdrieonians	L	0-1		14,000
30		29	(h)	Heart of Midlothian	W	4-1	Dalglish 2, Wilson, Glavin	21,000
31	Apr	5	(h)	Morton	D	1-1	Wilson	13,000
32		12	(a)	Dunfermline A	W	3-1	Wilson 2, Lennox	10,500
33		19	(h)	Dundee	L	1-2	Glavin	13,000
34		26	(a)	St. Johnstone	L	1-2	Glavin	11,000

FINAL LEAGUE POSITION : 3rd in Division One

Appearances

Sub. Appearances

Goals

Appearance grid (shirt numbers worn by each player per match). Columns are players; the final column is the match number.

Connaghan	McGrain	McCluskey P	Connelly	McNeill	Callaghan	Johnstone	Murray	Dalglish	Davidson	Wilson	Brogan J	Lennox	Hood	Deans	Hunter	MacDonald	Bone	Glavin	Welsh	Lynch	Latchford	McNamara	McLaughlin	Burns	#
1	2	3	4	5	6	7	8	9	10	11															1
1	2	6	4	5	13	7†	8	9*	10	11	3	12													2
1	2	4		5	6	7*	8	9	10	11	3	12													3
1	2	3		5	6	7	4	9		11		10	8												4
1	2	6		5	10	13	4	8†		11*	3	12	7	9											5
	2	12		5*		7	4	8		11	3		10	9	1	6									6
	2	6			10	7	4	8		11	3			9	1	5									7
	2	6		5		7	4	8		11	3*		10	9	1	12									8
		6		5		7*	4	8		11	3	12	10	9	1	2									9
		6		5	10		4	8		11	3		7	9	1	2									10
		6		5		4	8		10*	11	3		7	9	1	2	12								11
	2	6		5*		13	4	7†		11	3	10		9	1	12		8							12
	2	6		5	13	12	4	7		11	3	10†		9*	1			8							13
1	2	6		5			4	7		11	3	10					9	8							14
	2	6†		5			4	7		11	3	10	12		1		9*	8	13						15
	2	3	6	5	10	7	4*	9		11		13			1	12		8†							16
	2	3	6	5	10	7	4	9*		11		12	8		1										17
	2		6	5	10		4	9		11	3		7		1			8							18
	2	3	6†	5	10	7		8*		11	13		12	9	1	4									19
	2	6		5	10	12	4	9		11	3		7*		1			8							20
	2	3		5		12	4	10		11			7	9*	1	6		8							21
	2		6	5	10		4	8		11	3		7	9	1										22
	2		6	5	10		4	8		11†	3		7	9*	1			12		13					23
	2		6	5	10	12	4	9		11*	3		7		1			8							24
	2	3	6			4	10		11			7	9		5			8			1				25
	2	3	6	5			4	10		11			7	9				8			1				26
	2	3	6	5	10			9		8			7			4				11	1				27
	2	3*		5	6†	7		9		12		10	13			4		8		11	1				28
	2	6			10	7		8		12	3	11	13	9*		4†		5			1				29
	2	3	4	5	6	7		9*		11			10					8		12	1				30
	2	3	6		12			8		11†		10	7	9*	5	4					1	13			31
	2	3		5			8	9		7		11				4		10		6	1				32
	2	3		5			8	9		7*		11				4		10		6	1		12		33
	2			5	10	7†	4	11			12	13	9*			6		8		3	1				34
6	30	28	15	30	19	15	28	33	4	31	19	9	21	18	18	12	2	19	1	5	10	1			
	1			3	6			2	1	5	6	1		3	1	1	1	2			1	1			
	3		1	2	5	8	16	2	13		5	8	9		1	5		2							

23

1975-76

1	Aug	30	(a)	Rangers	L	1-2	Dalglish	69,594
2	Sep	6	(h)	Dundee	W	4-0	Lennox 3, McNamara	25,000
3		13	(a)	Motherwell	D	1-1	Dalglish	18,612
4		20	(a)	St. Johnstone	W	2-1	McCluskey P 2 (2 pens)	12,000
5		27	(h)	Dundee U	W	2-1	Dalglish, MacDonald	21,000
6	Oct	4	(h)	Heart of Midlothian	W	3-1	Deans, Hood, Wilson	20,000
7		11	(a)	Aberdeen	W	2-1	Dalglish, Deans	18,000
8	Nov	1	(h)	Rangers	D	1-1	Wilson	55,000
9		8	(a)	Dundee	L	0-1		16,456
10		12	(a)	Ayr U	W	7-2	Edvaldsson 3, Deans 2, Dalglish, MacDonald	15,000
11		15	(h)	Motherwell	L	0-2		33,000
12		22	(h)	St. Johnstone	W	3-2	Lennox 2, Dalglish	20,000
13		29	(a)	Dundee U	W	3-1	Deans, Lennox, Lynch	11,000
14	Dec	6	(a)	Heart of Midlothian	W	1-0	Deans	21,000
15		10	(h)	Hibernian	D	1-1	Deans	21,000
16		13	(h)	Aberdeen	L	0-2		24,000
17		20	(a)	Hibernian	W	3-1	Edvaldsson, Deans, McNamara	21,360
18		27	(h)	Ayr U	W	3-1	Edvaldsson 2, Dalglish	22,000
19	Jan	1	(a)	Rangers	L	0-1		57,839
20		3	(h)	Dundee	D	3-3	Dalglish 2, Deans	21,000
21		10	(a)	Motherwell	W	3-1	Deans 2, Dalglish	18,092
22		17	(a)	St. Johnstone	W	4-3	Dalglish, Deans, MacDonald, Edvaldsson	9,915
23		31	(h)	Dundee U	W	2-1	Dalglish, Wilson	18,000
24	Feb	7	(h)	Heart of Midlothian	W	2-0	Dalglish 2	22,000
25		21	(a)	Aberdeen	W	1-0	Lennox	18,221
26		28	(h)	Hibernian	W	4-0	Dalglish, Lennox, Wilson, Deans (pen)	33,000
27	Mar	20	(a)	Dundee	W	1-0	Dalglish	14,830
28		27	(h)	Motherwell	W	4-0	Dalglish 2, Lennox, Deans	29,000
29	Apr	3	(h)	St. Johnstone	W	1-0	Dalglish	16,000
30		10	(a)	Dundee U	L	2-3	Dalglish 2	12,771
31		17	(h)	Aberdeen	D	1-1	Dalglish	29,000
32		21	(a)	Hibernian	L	0-2		17,480
33		24	(h)	Ayr U	L	1-2	Deans (pen)	16,000
34		26	(h)	Rangers	D	0-0		51,000
35	May	1	(a)	Ayr U	W	5-3	Dalglish 2, Ritchie, Lennox, McCluskey P (pen)	6,800
36		3	(a)	Heart of Midlothian	L	0-1		9,000

FINAL LEAGUE POSITION : 2nd in Premier Division

Appearances

Sub. Appearances

Goals

Latchford	McGrain	Lynch	McCluskey P	MacDonald	Edvaldsson	McNamara	Wilson	Dalglish	Callaghan	Lennox	Connelly	Ritchie	Glavin	Hood	Deans	McCluskey G	Murray	Hunter	Casey	Aitken	Doyle	Burns	Hannah	No.
1	2	3	4	5	6	7*	8	9	10	11†	12	13												1
1	2	3	4*	5	6		8	9	10	11		12	7											2
1	2	3		5	6	8	7*	9	10	11			4	12										3
1	2*	3	4	5	6	7		8	10	11				12	9									4
1	2	3	4	5	6	7		9	10	11			8*	12										5
1	2	3	4	5	6	7*	8	10	12	11					9									6
1	2	3	4	5	6	7	8	10	12			13	11†		9*									7
1	2	3	4	5	6		11	8	10					12	9	7*								8
1	2	3	4	5	6	10	8	11	7*						9	12								9
1	2	3	4	5	6	10	7	8		11					9									10
1	2	3	4	5	6	10	7	8		11*				12	9									11
1	2	3	4	5	6			8	10	11			7		9									12
1	2	3	4	5	6	7	8	10		11					9									13
1	2	3	4	5	6		12	8	10	11			7*		9									14
1	2	3	4	5	6	12		8	10	11			7*		9									15
1	2	3	4	5	6	7*	8	10		11				12	9									16
1	2	3	6	5	4	7	8	10		11					9									17
1	2	3	6	5	4	7	8	10		11					9									18
1	2	3	6	5	4	7	12	8	10	11†			13		9*									19
1	2	3	6	5*	4	7	11†	8	10	13					9		12							20
1	2	6	3	5	4			10	11				7		9		8							21
1	2	6	3	5	4			10	11				7		9		8							22
	2	3	6		5	10	7	8		11*			4	12	9			1						23
1	2	3	4	5	11	10	7	8							9				6					24
1	2	3	4		6	11		8	12			7*	10		9					5				25
1	2	3	4		6	7		8		11			10		9					5				26
1	2	3	4	9	6		8	12	10	11										5	7*			27
1	2	3	4	9*	6		8	12	10	11			7							5				28
1	2	3	4	9*	6		8	12	10	11			7							5				29
1	2	3	4		6		12	8	10	11			7		9*					5				30
1	2		3	13	8	6	11†	12		4					9					5	7*	10		31
1	2	3	4		6	7*		8	10	11					9		12			5				32
1	2	3	4		6			8	10	11					9					5	7	11		33
1	2	3	4	9	6*		12	8		11										5	7	10		34
1	2	3	4		6			8		11					9					5	7	10*	12	35
1	2		6	10†	4	12		3	7	8					9*					5		11	13	36
35	35	34	34	27	35	16	18	35	22	25	1	5	10	7	29	2	2	1	1	12	5	5		
						2	8			5	2	3		7		2	1					2		
		1	3	3	7	2	4	24		10		1		1	15									

1976-77

1	Sep	4	(h)	Rangers	D	2-2	Wilson 2	57,000
2		11	(a)	Dundee U	L	0-1		15,000
3		18	(h)	Heart of Midlothian	D	2-2	Glavin, McCluskey G	27,000
4		25	(a)	Kilmarnock	W	4-0	Glavin, Craig, Doyle, MacDonald	14,900
5	Oct	2	(h)	Hibernian	D	1-1	Dalglish (pen)	29,000
6		16	(a)	Ayr U	W	2-0	Glavin, Craig	12,871
7		20	(h)	Dundee U	W	5-1	Glavin 3, Craig, Lennox	23,000
8		23	(a)	Aberdeen	L	1-2	Dalglish (pen)	19,370
9		30	(h)	Motherwell	W	2-0	Dalglish 2	31,000
10	Nov	20	(a)	Heart of Midlothian	W	4-3	Dalglish, MacDonald, Lennox, Glavin	20,500
11		24	(a)	Rangers	W	1-0	Craig	43,500
12		27	(h)	Kilmarnock	W	2-1	Craig, Wilson	22,000
13	Dec	18	(h)	Ayr U	W	3-0	Doyle, Wilson, Dalglish	18,000
14		26	(h)	Aberdeen	D	2-2	Craig 2	47,000
15	Jan	8	(a)	Dundee U	W	2-1	Dalglish, Doyle	16,000
16		11	(h)	Rangers	W	1-0	Jackson (og)	52,000
17		22	(a)	Kilmarnock	W	3-1	Glavin 2 (1 pen), Wilson	14,363
18	Feb	5	(h)	Hibernian	W	4-2	Glavin 2, Edvaldsson, Craig	28,000
19		7	(h)	Heart of Midlothian	W	5-1	Glavin (pen), Edvaldsson, Craig, Dalglish, Lynch	21,000
20		12	(h)	Partick Thistle	W	2-0	Glavin, Dalglish	26,000
21		19	(a)	Ayr U	W	4-2	Dalglish 2, Craig, Lynch	13,684
22		22	(a)	Partick Thistle	W	4-2	Edvaldsson, Glavin (pen), Craig, Aitken	13,000
23	Mar	5	(a)	Aberdeen	L	0-2		21,656
24		9	(h)	Partick Thistle	W	2-1	Conn, Doyle	22,000
25		16	(h)	Motherwell	D	2-2	Glavin (pen), Edvaldsson	23,000
26		19	(a)	Rangers	D	2-2	Aitken 2	51,500
27		26	(h)	Dundee U	W	2-0	Glavin (pen), Craig	37,000
28		30	(a)	Hibernian	D	1-1	Glavin	11,841
29	Apr	2	(a)	Heart of Midlothian	W	3-0	Glavin, Craig, Aitken	17,000
30		9	(h)	Kilmarnock	W	1-0	Craig	20,000
31		13	(a)	Motherwell	L	0-3		13,820
32		16	(a)	Hibernian	W	1-0	Craig	22,306
33		20	(a)	Aberdeen	W	4-1	Glavin, Conn, Craig, Dalglish	27,000
34		23	(a)	Partick Thistle	D	1-1	Aitken	18,000
35		30	(h)	Ayr U	W	2-0	Dalglish, Edvaldsson	17,000
36	May	10	(a)	Motherwell	D	2-2	Dalglish, Burns	12,500

FINAL LEAGUE POSITION : 1st in Premier Division

Appearances

Sub. Appearances

Goals

Latchford	McGrain	Lynch	Stanton	MacDonald	McCluskey P	Doyle	Glavin	Wilson	Burns	Dalglish	Lennox	Aitken	Craig	McCluskey G	Callaghan	Gibson	Edvaldsson	Conn	Baines	No.
1	2	3	4	5	6	7	8	9	10	11										1
1	2	3	4	5	6	7	8	9*	10	11	12									2
1	2	3	6			7	4	11*	10	8		5	9	12						3
1	2	3	4	5		11	8	12	10†	7		6*	9	13						4
1	2	3	4	5		11	8	12	10	7		6	9*							5
1	2	3	4	5		7	8	11		10		6	9							6
1	2	3	4	5		7*	8	11†	13	10	12	6	9							7
1	2	3	4	5		7	8	11		10		6	9							8
1	2	3	4	5		7	8	11		10		6	9							9
1	2	3	4	5		7	8			10	11	6	9							10
1	2	3	4	5		7	8	12		10	11*	6	9							11
1	2	3	4	5		7	8	11		10		6	9							12
1	2	3	4	5		7*	8†	11		10		6	9		12	13				13
1	2		4	5		7	8	11	3	10		6	9							14
1	2	3	4	5		7	8	11		10		6	9							15
1	2	3	4	5		7	8	11		10		6	9							16
1	2	3	4	5	12	7†	8	11		10		6*	9	13						17
1	2	3	4	5*		7	8	11		10		6	9			12				18
1	2	3	4		12	7	8	11	13	10		6*	9†				5			19
1	2	3	4		12	7	8	11*		10		6	9				5			20
1	2	3	4			7	8	11*	12	10		6	9				5			21
1	2	3	4		13	7*	8	11†	12	10		6	9				5			22
1	2	3	4		6*	7	8			11	10		9				5	12		23
1	2		4			7	8		3	10		6	9				5	11		24
1	2		4			7	8		3	10		6	9				5	11		25
1	2		4			7	8		3	10		6	9				5	11		26
	2		4			7	8		3	10		6	9				5	11	1	27
	2		4			7	8		3	10		6	9			7	5	11	1	28
	2	3	4	5		7*	8	12		10		6	9†		13			11	1	29
	2	3	4	5		7†	8	13		12		6*	9			10		11	1	30
	2	3	4				8	11		10		6	9				5	7	1	31
1	2	3	4	5		7	8*	12		10		6	9				11			32
1	2	3	4	5		7	8			10		6	9				11			33
1	2	3	4	5		7*	8†	12	13	10		6	9				11			34
1	2	3	4	5		7				10	8	6	9†	13			12	11*		35
1	2	3	4	5	13			11†	12	7		6	9				8*	10		36
31	36	30	36	24	4	33	34	19	13	35	2	33	34		1	13	13	5		
				4		1		5	9		3			1	1	2	4	1		
	2		2		4	19	5	1	14	2	5	16	1				5	2		

27

1977-78

#	Month	Date		Opponent	Res	Score	Scorers	Attendance
1	Aug	13	(h)	Dundee U	D	0-0		34,000
2		20	(a)	Ayr U	L	1-2	Craig	14,500
3		27	(h)	Motherwell	L	0-1		29,000
4	Sep	10	(a)	Rangers	L	2-3	Edvaldsson 2	48,788
5		17	(a)	Aberdeen	L	1-2	Garner (og)	25,800
6		24	(h)	Clydebank	W	1-0	McAdam	20,000
7	Oct	1	(h)	Hibernian	W	3-1	Edvaldsson, Glavin, Craig	26,000
8		8	(a)	Partick Thistle	L	0-1		19,500
9		15	(h)	St. Mirren	L	1-2	McAdam	29,000
10		22	(a)	Dundee U	W	2-1	Glavin (pen), Wilson	17,000
11		29	(h)	Ayr U	W	3-2	McAdam, Glavin, MacDonald	20,000
12	Nov	5	(a)	Motherwell	W	3-2	Craig 2, MacDonald	16,547
13		12	(h)	Rangers	D	1-1	McAdam	56,000
14		19	(h)	Aberdeen	W	3-2	Aitken, Edvaldsson, Lynch (pen)	27,000
15	Dec	10	(h)	Partick Thistle	W	3-0	McAdam, MacDonald, Lynch (pen)	27,000
16		17	(a)	St. Mirren	D	3-3	McAdam, Craig, Lynch (pen)	17,800
17		24	(h)	Dundee U	W	1-0	Edvaldsson	21,000
18		31	(a)	Ayr U	L	1-2	Edvaldsson	14,000
19	Jan	2	(h)	Motherwell	L	0-1		23,000
20		7	(a)	Rangers	L	1-3	Edvaldsson	51,000
21		14	(a)	Aberdeen	L	1-2	MacDonald	24,600
22	Feb	25	(h)	St. Mirren	L	1-2	McCluskey	22,000
23	Mar	4	(a)	Dundee U	W	1-0	Narey (og)	12,771
24		11	(h)	Ayr U	W	3-0	Edvaldsson, Glavin, McCluskey	15,000
25		22	(a)	Motherwell	L	1-2	Craig	9,613
26		25	(h)	Rangers	W	2-0	Glavin, MacDonald	50,000
27		29	(a)	Partick Thistle	W	4-0	Burns 2, MacDonald, McAdam	12,000
28	Apr	1	(h)	Aberdeen	D	2-2	Glavin, Edvaldsson	24,000
29		5	(h)	Hibernian	W	2-1	McCluskey 2	20,000
30		8	(a)	Clydebank	L	2-3	McCluskey, Burns	8,500
31		12	(a)	Hibernian	D	1-1	McCluskey	10,902
32		15	(a)	Hibernian	L	1-4	Conroy	16,286
33		17	(h)	Clydebank	W	5-2	Edvaldsson, Aitken, McAdam, Glavin, MacDonald	7,000
34		22	(h)	Partick Thistle	W	5-2	Doyle 2, Craig 2, Glavin	16,000
35		26	(a)	Clydebank	D	1-1	Conroy	4,000
36		29	(a)	St. Mirren	L	1-3	Glavin (pen)	13,026

FINAL LEAGUE POSITION : 5th in Premier Division

Appearances

Sub. Appearances

Goals

Latchford	McGrain	Lynch	Stanton	MacDonald	Aitken	Glavin	Edvaldsson	Craig	Burns	Conn	Doyle	Lennox	Kay	Wilson	Casey	Dowie	McAdam	McWilliams	McLaughlin	Munro	Fillipi	McCluskey G	Sneddon	Conroy	Mackie	No.
1	2	3	4*	5	6	7	8	9	10	11†	12	13														1
1	2			5	4	7*	8	9	6		12	10	3	11†	13											2
1	2			5	6	7	8	9	10		11		3		4											3
1	2	3		5		9	4		10†		7	13		11	6	8*	12									4
1	2	3		5	10	7	4	9*			12			11		8	6									5
1	2	3		5	6	8	4	10*			7			11		12	9									6
1	2			5	6	7	4	9	11			3	8		10											7
1		3		5	6	4	12	9*	10			2	11		8		7									8
1				5	10	9	4		3	11		2	7		8		6									9
1		3		5	2	4	12	9*	10		7			11		8	6									10
1		3		5	2	4	8		10		7			11		9	6									11
1		3		5	4		12	9	10*		7			11		8	6	2								12
1		3		5	6	8	4	9*		11	7			12		10		2								13
1		3		5	6		8	9*		11	7			12		10	4	2								14
1		3		5	6		8	10		11	7					9	4	2								15
1		3		5	6	8*	4	10		11†	7			13		12	9	2								16
1		3		5	4		8	10		11*	7			12		6	9	2								17
1		3		5	4		8	10*		11	7					9	6	2	12							18
1		3		5	10	8	4			7*				11		9	6	2	12							19
1		3		5	4	7	8	9						11		10	6	2								20
1		3		5	4	7	8		12					11*		10	6	2	9							21
1				5	10		7*		3	11†				13	12	8		4	6	9	2					22
1				5	6		8	9	10							3	11	4*	12	7	2					23
1				5	6	7	8		11							3	10		4	9	2					24
1		3		5	6	7	8	9						10	11			4		2						25
1		3		5	4	7	8		10	11						6	9				2					26
1		3		5	4	7	8		10	11						6	9				2					27
1		3		5	4	7	8		10	11*						6	9		12		2					28
1				5	3	7	8		6	11						4	10				9	2				29
1	3*			5†	4	7	8		11	12						6	10		13		9	2				30
1				5	4	7	8		3	11*				12		6	10				9	2				31
1	12			5	4		8		3		13			11†		6*	10				9	2	7			32
1		3		5	4	7	8		6*	12						9					11	2	10			33
1		3		5		8	4	9		11						10					7	2	6			34
1		3		5		8	4	9		11*						10					7	2	6	12		35
1	3*			5	6	7	4	12								9					11	2	10	8		36
36	7	26	1	36	33	28	33	19	22	9	20	1	5	14	2	12	32	1	1	14	11	12	15	5	1	
	1				3	1	1	1	5	2		6	2	2	1			1	1	3			1			
	3			7	2	9	10	8	3		2			1		8					6		2			

1978-79

1	Aug	12	(a)	Morton	W	2-1	Glavin, MacDonald	16,000
2		19	(h)	Hearts	W	4-0	Conn 2, Burns, McAdam	25,000
3		26	(a)	Motherwell	W	5-1	Conn 2, Aitken 2, McAdam	19,710
4	Sep	9	(h)	Rangers	W	3-1	McAdam 2, McCluskey	60,000
5		16	(h)	Hibernian	L	0-1		27,000
6		23	(a)	Partick Thistle	W	3-2	Lynch (pen), Aitken, MacDonald	23,000
7		30	(h)	St. Mirren	W	2-1	Lynch (pen), Conn	26,000
8	Oct	7	(a)	Aberdeen	L	1-4	McAdam	25,000
9		14	(a)	Dundee U	L	0-1		17,726
10		21	(h)	Morton	D	0-0		24,000
11		28	(a)	Hearts	L	0-2		18,500
12	Nov	4	(h)	Motherwell	L	1-2	McAdam	21,000
13		11	(a)	Rangers*	D	1-1	Lynch	52,330
14		18	(a)	Hibernian	D	2-2	Provan, MacLeod	22,000
15		25	(h)	Partick Thistle	W	1-0	McAdam	26,000
16	Dec	9	(h)	Aberdeen	D	0-0		24,000
17		16	(h)	Dundee U	D	1-1	Lynch (pen)	21,000
18		23	(a)	Morton	L	0-1		13,000
19	Mar	3	(h)	Aberdeen	W	1-0	Conn	26,000
20		17	(h)	Motherwell	W	2-1	Lennox 2	16,000
21		28	(h)	Morton	W	3-0	Provan, Burns, Glavin	16,000
22		31	(a)	Hibernian	L	1-2	Glavin (pen)	18,000
23	Apr	4	(a)	Motherwell	W	4-3	Doyle, Lennox (pen), McGrain, Davidson	8,744
24		7	(h)	Partick Thistle	W	2-0	Conroy, Lynch	19,000
25		11	(a)	Dundee U	L	1-2	Davidson	14,424
26		14	(a)	St. Mirren	W	1-0	McCluskey	19,721
27		18	(a)	Hearts	W	3-0	MacLeod, Conroy, Burns	21,000
28		21	(h)	Aberdeen	D	1-1	Lynch (pen)	19,400
29		25	(h)	St. Mirren	W	2-1	Edvaldsson, Aitken	18,000
30		28	(h)	Dundee U	W	2-1	Doyle, Lynch (pen)	37,000
31	May	2	(h)	Hibernian	W	3-1	Conroy, Provan, McGrain	23,000
32		5	(a)	Rangers*	L	0-1		52,841
33		7	(a)	Partick Thistle	W	2-1	Provan, McCluskey	18,000
34		11	(a)	St. Mirren†	W	2-0	Lennox, McCluskey	22,000
35		14	(h)	Hearts	W	1-0	Conroy	18,000
36		21	(h)	Rangers	W	4-2	Aitken, McCluskey, MacLeod, Jackson (og)	52,000

FINAL LEAGUE POSITION : 1st in Premier Division

Appearances

Sub. Appearances

Goals

Latchford	Fillipi	Sneddon	Aitken	MacDonald	Edvaldsson	Doyle	Glavin	McAdam	Burns	Conn	Casey	Lynch	Wilson	Conroy	McCluskey G	Craig	Provan	Lennox	Mackie	Baines	MacLeod	McGrain	Bonner	Davidson	
1	2	3	4	5	6	7*	8	9	10	11	12														1
1	2		4	5	6	7*	8	9	10†	11	13	3	12												2
1	2		4	5	6	7	8	9	10	11		3													3
1	2		4		5	7	6	9	10*		12	3		8	11†	13									4
1	2		4		5	12	6*	9	10	7		3		8	11										5
1	2		4	5	6			9	10	8		3		12	11*	7									6
1	2		4		5		6	9	10	11		3		8		7									7
1	2	3	4	5	6*		12	9	10†					8	11	7	13								8
1	2		4	5	6*			9		3	10†			8	13	7	11	12							9
1	2	3	4	5	6			9	10*					8	12	7	11								10
1	2		4	5	6			9	10*	8					11	7		12							11
	2		4	5	6			9	10	11		3				7			1		8				12
	2		4	5	6	11		9	10			3				7			1		8				13
	2*		4	5	6	11		9		12		3			10†	7	13		1		8				14
	2		4	5	6	11		9	10			3				7			1		8				15
	2		4	5	6	11	9*	10		12		3				7			1		8				16
	2		4	5	6	11	10	9*									12		1		8				17
	2		4	5	6			9	10*	11		3				7	12		1		8				18
1	12		4	5	6	11		10*	9			3				7					8	2			19
			4	5	6	11		12	10			3				7	9				8*	2	1		20
1	3		4	5*	6	11	8		10						12	7	9					2			21
1	3		4		5	11	8		10					6*	13	7†	12					2		9	22
			4		5	11			10					6		7	8				3	2	1	9	23
1			4		5	11			10			3		8		7					6	2		9	24
1			4		5	13			10			3		8*	12	7	11†				6	2		9	25
1			4		5	9						3		8	11	7					6	2		10	26
1			4		5	9		12				3		9	11	7*					6	2		10	27
1			4		5	13		12	10			3		8	11†	7					6	2		9*	28
1			4		5	11			10			3		8		7					6	2		9	29
1			4		5	11			10			3		8	9	7					6	2			30
1			4		5	11			10					6	9	7					3	2		8	31
1			4		5	11		12	10†			13		6	9	7					3	2		8*	32
1			4			11		5				3		8	9	7					6	2		10	33
1			4			11		5	10			3			9	7	12				6	2		8*	34
1			4		6	11		5				3*		8	9	7	12				10	2			35
1			4		6	11		5				3		8*	9	7	12				10	2			36
27	19	4	36	18	34	23	9	24	28	12	1	27		20	16	30	6		7		23	18	2	12	
	1					2	1	4	1	1	4	1	1	1	5	1					8	2			
		5	2	1	2	3	7	3	6		7			4	5		4	4			3	2		2	

1979-80

1	Aug	11	(h)	Morton	W	3-2	McCluskey, Provan, MacLeod (pen)	26,000
2		18	(a)	Rangers	D	2-2	Sneddon, McAdam	36,000
3		25	(h)	Kilmarnock	W	5-0	McCluskey 3 (1 pen), Davidson 2	26,000
4	Sep	8	(h)	Dundee U	D	2-2	McCluskey 2	27,000
5		15	(a)	Hibernian	W	3-1	Lennox, Conroy, MacLeod (pen)	18,000
6		22	(a)	Aberdeen	W	2-1	Aitken, Doyle	23,000
7		29	(h)	St. Mirren	W	3-1	MacLeod, MacDonald, McAdam	29,000
8	Oct	6	(a)	Partick Thistle	D	0-0		21,000
9		13	(h)	Dundee	W	3-0	McAdam 2, MacLeod (pen)	25,000
10		20	(a)	Morton	L	0-1		18,000
11		27	(h)	Rangers	W	1-0	MacDonald	56,000
12	Nov	3	(a)	Kilmarnock	L	0-2		18,000
13		10	(a)	Dundee U	W	1-0	Edvaldsson	18,630
14		17	(h)	Hibernian	W	3-0	Edvaldsson 2, Lennox	25,000
15	Dec	1	(a)	St. Mirren	L	1-2	MacDonald	20,500
16		15	(h)	Partick Thistle	W	5-1	McAdam 2, MacDonald, Lennox, Sullivan	19,000
17		22	(h)	Morton	W	3-1	McAdam, Sullivan, Doyle	27,000
18		29	(a)	Rangers	D	1-1	Lennox	34,500
19	Jan	5	(h)	Dundee U	W	1-0	MacLeod (pen)	25,000
20		12	(a)	Hibernian	D	1-1	Aitken	21,936
21		19	(a)	Aberdeen	D	0-0		24,000
22	Feb	9	(a)	Partick Thistle	D	1-1	MacLeod	17,000
23		23	(h)	Dundee	D	2-2	MacLeod, McCluskey	23,000
24	Mar	1	(a)	Morton	W	1-0	Doyle	20,000
25		12	(h)	St. Mirren	D	2-2	Doyle, McCluskey	30,000
26		15	(a)	Kilmarnock	D	1-1	Lennox	15,000
27		29	(h)	Hibernian	W	4-0	Lennox (pen), Doyle, McGarvey, MacDonald	22,000
28	Apr	2	(h)	Rangers	W	1-0	McGarvey	52,000
29		5	(h)	Aberdeen	L	1-2	Doyle	40,000
30		8	(a)	Dundee U	L	0-3		14,616
31		16	(h)	Kilmarnock	W	2-0	MacDonald, Doyle	18,000
32		19	(a)	Dundee	L	1-5	Aitken	14,633
33		23	(h)	Aberdeen	L	1-3	McCluskey (pen)	48,000
34		26	(h)	Partick Thistle	W	2-1	McCluskey, McAdam	20,000
35		30	(a)	Dundee	W	2-0	Conroy, Sullivan	10,200
36	May	3	(a)	St. Mirren	D	0-0		20,166

FINAL LEAGUE POSITION : 2nd in Premier Division

Appearances

Sub. Appearances

Goals

Latchford	Sneddon	McGrain	Aitken	MacDonald	McAdam	Provan	Conroy	McCluskey G	MacLeod	Burns	Lennox	Edvaldsson	Doyle	Davidson	Casey	Lynch	Sullivan	McGarvey	
1	2	3	4	5	6	7	8	9	10	11*	12								1
1	2	3	4	5	11	7	8	9*	10		13	6†	12						2
1	2	3	4*	5	6	7		9	10		12		11	8					3
1	2	3	4		5	7	6*	9	10		12		11	8					4
1	2	3	4	12	5	7	6	9*	10		11			8					5
1	2	3	4	5	6		8		10	11	9		7						6
1	2	3	4	5	6	7		9*	10		12		11	8					7
1	2	3*	4			7	6	9	10		13	5	11	8†	12				8
1	2	3	4	5	6	7		9	10	11	12		8*						9
1	2		4	5	6	7*	12	9	10	11	8				3				10
1	2	3	4	5	11	7	13	9*	6	10†		12					8		11
1	2	3	4	5	9*	7	12		6	10		13	11†				8		12
1	2	3	4		5	7	10		6		11	9					8		13
1	2	3	4		5	7	10		6		11	9					8		14
1	2	3	4	13	5	7	10†	11	6		12	9*					8		15
1	2	3	4	5	6	7*	12	9	10	11							8		16
1	2	3	4	5	6	7		9*	10	11		12					8		17
1	2	3	4	5	6	7			10	9		11					8		18
1	2	3	4	5	6	7			10	9	12	11*					8		19
1	2	3	4	5	6	7			10	9		11					8		20
1	2	3	4	5	6	7			10	9		11					8		21
1	2	3	4	5	6	7	12		10	9		11					8*		22
1	2	3	4	5		7		8	6	9		11				10			23
1	2	3		5	4	7		8	6	9		11	10						24
1	2	3	4	5	6	7		8	10			11						9	25
1	2	3	4	5	6	7		8*	10		12	11						9	26
1		2	4	5	6	7	13	3	12	10		11†			8*			9	27
1	2	3	4	5	6	7			10		8	11						9	28
1	2	3	4	5	6*	7			10	11	12	8						9	29
1	2	3	4	5	6	7		8*	10	12	11	13						9†	30
1	2		4	5	6	7			3	10	8	11						9	31
1	2*	3	4	5	6	7			10	12	8	11						9	32
1		2	4	5	6	7	8*	9	3	10		11						12	33
1		2	4		5	7	6	9	3	10							8	11	34
1		2	4		5	7	6	9	3	10							8	11	35
1	2	3	4		5	7	8	9	6	10							11		36
36	32	34	35	27	34	35	13	22	36	12	19	5	22	5	2	1	15	11	
				2			5	1		3	10	4	2		1			1	
	1		3	6	8	1	2	10	7		6	3	7	2			3	2	

33

1980-81

1	Aug	9	(h)	Morton	W	2-1	McCluskey, MacLeod		20,000
2		16	(a)	Kilmarnock	W	3-0	McGarvey 2, Sullivan		13,800
3		23	(h)	Rangers	L	1-2	Burns		58,000
4	Sep	6	(h)	Partick Thistle	W	4-1	Nicholas 2, McGarvey, MacLeod (pen)		20,000
5		13	(a)	Hearts	W	2-0	Nicholas, Provan		17,169
6		20	(h)	Airdrie	D	1-1	Nicholas (pen)		18,000
7		27	(a)	Aberdeen	D	2-2	Nicholas (pen), Burns		23,000
8	Oct	4	(h)	Dundee U	W	2-0	Nicholas, McGarvey		21,000
9		11	(a)	St. Mirren	W	2-0	McCormack (og), Stark (og)		18,601
10		18	(a)	Morton	W	3-2	Nicholas, Provan, Aitken		16,000
11		25	(h)	Kilmarnock	W	4-1	Nicholas (2 pens), McGarvey 2		18,000
12	Nov	1	(a)	Rangers	L	0-3			33,000
13		8	(h)	Aberdeen	L	0-2			29,000
14		15	(a)	Airdrie	W	4-1	Nicholas, Aitken, McGarvey, McAdam		15,000
15		22	(h)	St. Mirren	L	1-2	McCluskey (pen)		16,000
16		29	(a)	Dundee U	W	3-0	McAdam, Weir, Hegarty (og)		15,000
17	Dec	6	(a)	Partick Thistle	W	1-0	McCluskey		12,436
18		13	(h)	Hearts	W	3-2	McCluskey, MacDonald, McGarvey		13,800
19		20	(h)	Airdrie	W	2-1	McCluskey, McAdam		11,900
20		27	(a)	Aberdeen	L	1-4	Nicholas		23,500
21	Jan	1	(a)	Kilmarnock	W	2-1	McGarvey 2		8,000
22		3	(h)	Morton	W	3-0	McGarvey 2, Provan		14,900
23		10	(h)	Dundee U	W	2-1	McGarvey, Nicholas		22,000
24		31	(a)	Hearts	W	3-0	McGarvey, Burns, Sullivan		14,596
25	Feb	21	(h)	Rangers	W	3-1	Nicholas 2, Aitken		52,800
26		28	(a)	Morton	W	3-0	McGarvey 2, Provan		14,000
27	Mar	14	(h)	St. Mirren	W	7-0	McGarvey 3, McCluskey 2, Aitken, Nicholas		18,000
28		18	(h)	Partick Thistle	W	4-1	McGarvey, MacLeod 2, Sullivan		15,000
29		21	(a)	Airdrie	W	2-1	McGarvey, MacLeod		13,000
30		28	(h)	Aberdeen	D	1-1	McCluskey		35,200
31	Apr	1	(h)	Hearts	W	6-0	McCluskey 2 (1 pen), MacLeod 2, McGarvey, Provan		13,300
32		5	(a)	Partick Thistle	W	1-0	McAdam		17,196
33		18	(a)	Rangers	W	1-0	Nicholas		34,000
34		22	(a)	Dundee U	W	3-2	McGarvey, MacLeod, Burns		15,349
35		25	(h)	Kilmarnock	D	1-1	Provan		22,200
36	May	2	(a)	St. Mirren	L	1-3	Provan		14,806

FINAL LEAGUE POSITION : 1st in Premier Division

Appearances

Sub. Appearances

Goals

Bonner	Sneddon	McGrain	Aitken	McAdam	Conroy	Provan	Sullivan	McGarvey	MacLeod	McCluskey G	Burns	Nicholas	Weir	Doyle	MacDonald	Reid	#
1	2	3	4	5	6*	7	8	9	10	11	12						1
1	2	3	4	5		7	8	9*	6	11	10	12					2
1	2	3	4	5		7	8	9	6	11	10						3
1	2	3	4	5		7	8	9*	6	12	10	11					4
1	2	3	4	5	12	7	8		6*	9	10	11					5
1	2	3		5	4	7	8			9*	10	11	6	12			6
1	2	3		4	6	7	8	9*	13		10†	11		12	5		7
1	2	3		6	4		8	9	10	7		11			5		8
1	2	3	4	6		7	8	9		10		11			5		9
1	2	3	4	6		7*	8		12	9		11		10	5		10
1	2	3	4	6		7	8	9			10	11			5		11
1	2	3	4	6		7	8	9*		12	10	11†		13	5		12
1	2	3	4	5	6*	7	8	9†		12	10	11		13			13
1		2	4	5		7		9		8	10	11	6			3	14
1		2	4	6			7	9		12	10	11*	8		5	3	15
1		2	4	6			7	9		11	10		8		5	3	16
1	2		4	6		12	7*	9		11	10		8		5	3	17
1	2		4	6		7		9		11	10		8		5	3	18
1		2	4	6		7		9		11	10		8		5	3	19
1		2	4	6	7*	12		9		11†	10	13	8		5	3	20
1		2	6	5		7	4	9			10	11	8			3	21
1		2	6	5		7	4	9			10	11	8			3	22
1		2	6	5		7	4	9			10	11	8			3	23
1		2	6	5	8	7	4	9		12	10	11*				3	24
1		2	6	5	8	7	4	9			10	11				3	25
1		2	6	5	8	7	4	9			10	11				3	26
1		2	6	5	8*	7	4	9	12	13	10	11†				3	27
1		2	6	5	8*	7	4	9	12		10	11				3	28
1		2	6	5		7	4	9	8		10	11				3	29
1		2	6	5		7	4	9	8	12	10	11*				3	30
1		2	6	5		7	4	9	8	11						3	31
1			6	5	8	7	4	9*	2	11	10	12				3	32
1		2	6	5	8	7		9	3		10	11		4			33
1		2	6	5	8	7		9	4		10	11				3	34
1		2	6	5		7	4	9	8		10	11				3	35
1		2	6			7	4	9	8		10	11		5		3	36
36	15	33	33	35	14	31	30	33	14	16	32	26	11	1	14	22	
					1	2			4	7	1	3			4		
		4	4		7	3		23	8	10	4	16	1		1		

35

1981-82

1	Aug	29	(h)	Airdrie	W 5-2	McCluskey 2, Burns, McGarvey, Nicholas	21,100
2	Sep	5	(a)	Aberdeen	W 3-1	McCluskey 2, Burns	18,825
3		12	(h)	Morton	W 2-1	MacLeod, McAdam	19,900
4		19	(a)	Rangers	W 2-0	McAdam, MacLeod	40,900
5		26	(h)	Partick Thistle	W 2-0	Nicholas, Burns	15,200
6	Oct	3	(a)	Dundee	W 3-1	McCluskey 2, McGarvey	13,254
7		10	(a)	St. Mirren	W 2-1	McCluskey, Nicholas	16,441
8		17	(h)	Dundee U	D 1-1	McCluskey	23,000
9		24	(a)	Hibernian	L 0-1		18,000
10		31	(a)	Airdrie	W 3-1	McCluskey (pen), Sullivan, Burns	13,500
11	Nov	7	(h)	Aberdeen	W 2-1	McCluskey, McGarvey	29,356
12		14	(a)	Morton	D 1-1	McCluskey	12,412
13		21	(h)	Rangers	D 3-3	McAdam, McGarvey, MacLeod	48,600
14		28	(a)	Partick Thistle	W 2-0	McCluskey, Provan	13,073
15	Dec	5	(h)	Dundee	W 3-1	McGarvey 2, Conroy	14,570
16	Jan	9	(a)	Rangers	L 0-1		42,000
17		30	(a)	Aberdeen	W 3-1	McCluskey (pen), MacLeod, P. McStay	20,000
18	Feb	2	(h)	Hibernian	D 0-0		16,700
19		6	(a)	Dundee	W 3-1	MacLeod 2, McGarvey	11,373
20		20	(h)	Partick Thistle	D 2-2	McCluskey, Aitken	14,200
21		27	(a)	Hibernian	L 0-1		15,914
22	Mar	3	(h)	Morton	W 1-0	McGarvey	9,000
23		13	(a)	St. Mirren	W 5-2	MacLeod 2, Burns, Sullivan, McCluskey	17,084
24		20	(h)	Airdrie	W 2-0	Sullivan, Burns	12,000
25		27	(h)	Aberdeen	L 0-1		30,080
26		31	(a)	Dundee U	W 2-0	Burns 2	15,143
27	Apr	3	(a)	Morton	D 1-1	Crainie	10,500
28		10	(h)	Rangers	W 2-1	Crainie, McAdam	49,144
29		14	(a)	Airdrie	W 5-1	Crainie, Aitken, McCluskey, Reid (pen), Provan	12,000
30		17	(h)	Dundee	W 4-2	McCluskey 2, Provan, Reid (pen)	14,288
31		21	(h)	Dundee U	W 3-1	McCluskey 2, Provan	14,659
32		24	(a)	Partick Thistle	W 3-0	Crainie 3	14,200
33	May	1	(h)	Hibernian	W 6-0	MacLeod 2, Crainie, McCluskey, Aitken, Burns	16,064
34		3	(h)	St. Mirren	D 0-0		27,395
35		8	(a)	Dundee U	L 0-3		16,779
36		15	(h)	St. Mirren	W 3-0	McCluskey 2, McAdam	39,669

FINAL LEAGUE POSITION : 1st in Premier Division

Appearances

Sub. Appearances

Goals

Bonner	McGrain	Reid	Aitken	Moyes	MacLeod	Provan	Sullivan	McGarvey	Burns	McCluskey G	Nicholas	McAdam	Garner	Conroy	McStay P	Halpin	Crainie	
1	2	3	4	5	6	7	8	9*	10	11	12							1
1	2	3	4		6	7	8	9	10	11		5						2
1	2	3	4		6	7	8	9	10	11		5						3
1	2	3	4		6	7	8	9	10	11		5						4
1	2*	3	4	12	6		8	9	10	11	7	5						5
1		3	4	2	6		8	9	10	11	7	5						6
1	2	3	4		6		8	9	10	11	7	5						7
1		3	4	2	6		8	9	10	11	7	5						8
1		3	4	2	6		8	9	10	11	7		5					9
1		3	4	2	6		8	9	10	11	7	5						10
1		3	4	2	6	7	8	9	10*	11		5		12				11
1		3	4	2	6	7	8	9*		11	12	5		10				12
1		3	4	2	6	7	8	9		11		5		10				13
1		3	4	2	6	7	8*	9		11	12	5		10				14
1	2	3	4		6	7		9	10	11		5		8				15
1	2	3	4	13	6	7*		12	10	11	9	5		8†				16
1	2	3	4		6		7	9	10	11		5			8			17
1	2	3	4		6		7*	9	10	11		5			8	12		18
1	2	3	4		6		7	9	10	11		5			8			19
1	2	3	4		6*			9	10	11		5		12	8	7†	13	20
1	2	3	4		6			9	10	11		5		8	7*		12	21
1	2	3	4		6	7		9	10	8		5			11			22
1	2	3	4		6		8	9*	11	10		5			12		7	23
1	2	3	4	5	6		8	9	11	10*	12						7	24
1	2	3*	4	12	6		8	9	11	10		5					7	25
1	2	3	4		6		8	9*	11	10		5			12		7	26
1		3	4	2	6	12	8*		11	10		5		9			7	27
1	2	3	4	5	6	7	8		11	9							10	28
1	2	3	4		6	7	8		11	9		5					10	29
1	2	3	4		6	7	8		10	9		5					11	30
1	2	3	4		6	7	8		10	9		5					11	31
1	2	3	4		6	7	8		10	9		5					11	32
1	2	3	4		6	7	8		10	11		5					9	33
1	2	3	4		6	7	8		10	9		5					11	34
1	2	3	4	13	6	7	8*		10	9†		5			12		11	35
1	2	3	4		6	7			10	9		5			8		11	36
36	27	36	33	15	36	19	31	25	33	35	7	33	1	6	7	2	14	
				4		1		1			3	1		2	3	1	2	
		2	3		10	4	3	10	9	21	3	5		1	1		7	

1982-83

1	Sep	4	(h)	Dundee	W	2-0	Provan, Aitken	19,122
2		11	(a)	St. Mirren	W	2-1	Nicholas 2 (2 pens)	15,449
3		18	(a)	Motherwell	W	7-0	Nicholas 3, Aitken 2, McGarvey, MacLeod	17,092
4		25	(h)	Hibernian	W	2-0	McStay, MacLeod	16,371
5	Oct	2	(a)	Dundee U	D	2-2	McStay, Aitken	20,000
6		9	(h)	Aberdeen	L	1-3	Nicholas	29,733
7		16	(h)	Kilmarnock	W	2-1	Nicholas 2	11,063
8		23	(a)	Morton	W	2-1	Nicholas (pen), McGarvey	12,000
9		30	(h)	Rangers	W	3-2	McStay, McGarvey, MacLeod	60,408
10	Nov	6	(a)	Dundee	W	3-2	Nicholas (pen), McGarvey, Burns	11,681
11		13	(h)	St. Mirren	W	5-0	Nicholas 3 (1 pen), Aitken, Burns	15,044
12		20	(h)	Motherwell	W	3-1	Nicholas, McStay, Burns	14,963
13		27	(a)	Hibernian	W	3-2	McGarvey 2, McStay	17,121
14	Dec	11	(a)	Aberdeen	W	2-1	MacLeod, Provan	25,000
15		18	(a)	Kilmarnock	W	4-0	Provan, McAdam, McGarvey, Burns	9,000
16		27	(h)	Morton	W	5-1	McGarvey 2, Nicholas (pen), MacLeod, Reid	19,953
17	Jan	1	(a)	Rangers	W	2-1	McStay, Nicholas	44,000
18		3	(h)	Dundee	D	2-2	Burns, Nicholas	16,615
19		8	(a)	St. Mirren	W	1-0	MacLeod	14,748
20		15	(a)	Motherwell	L	1-2	MacLeod	15,290
21		22	(h)	Hibernian	W	4-1	McGarvey 2, Nicholas, McCluskey	17,106
22	Feb	5	(a)	Dundee U	D	1-1	Nicholas	17,289
23		12	(h)	Aberdeen	L	1-3	Nicholas	42,831
24		26	(h)	Kilmarnock	W	4-0	McGarvey 2, Nicholas (pen), MacLeod	10,691
25	Mar	5	(a)	Morton	W	3-0	Sullivan, MacLeod, McCluskey	8,500
26		19	(a)	Dundee	L	1-2	McGarvey	11,196
27		23	(h)	Rangers	D	0-0		51,062
28		26	(h)	St. Mirren	D	1-1	Provan	15,935
29	Apr	2	(h)	Motherwell	W	3-0	McGarvey, McAdam, Harrow (og)	15,454
30		6	(h)	Dundee U	W	2-0	McGarvey, Nicholas	34,508
31		9	(a)	Hibernian	W	3-0	Nicholas 2, Provan	15,500
32		20	(h)	Dundee U	L	2-3	Nicholas (pen), Burns	23,965
33		23	(a)	Aberdeen	L	0-1		24,500
34		30	(a)	Kilmarnock	W	5-0	MacLeod 2, McGrain, Nicholas, Burns	7,900
35	May	7	(h)	Morton	W	2-0	Nicholas (pen), Aitken	12,610
36		14	(a)	Rangers	W	4-2	Nicholas 2 (2 pens), McAdam, McGarvey	39,000

FINAL LEAGUE POSITION : 2nd in Premier League

Appearances

Sub. Appearances

Goals

38

Bonner	McGrain	Reid	Aitken	McAdam	MacLeod	Provan	McStay P	McCluskey G	Burns	Nicholas	Craine	McGarvey	Moyes	Sullivan	Sinclair	McInally J	McStay W	
1	2	3	4	5	6	7	8	9	10	11								1
1	2	3	4	5	6		8	9*	10	11	7	12						2
1	2	3	4	5	10	7	8	13		11†	12	9*	6					3
1	2	3	4	5	6	7	8	12		11		9*		10				4
1	2	3	4	5	10	7	8	12		11		9*			6			5
1	2	3	4	5	10*	7	8			11	12	9			6			6
1		3	4	5	10	7	8			11	9	12		6	2*			7
1	2	3	4	5	10	7	8			11	12	9*			6			8
1	2	3	4	5	10	7	8			11		9			6			9
1	2		4	5	10	7	8		6	11		9			3			10
1	2		4	5	10	7	8	12	6	11		9*			3			11
1	2		4	5	10	7	8	12	6	11		9*			3			12
1	2		4	5		7	8		10	11		9	6		3			13
1	2		4	5	6	7	8		10	11		9			3			14
1	2		4	5	6	7*	8	12	10	11		9			3			15
1	2	13		5	6	7	8	12	10	11		9*	4†		3			16
1	2	3		5	6	7	8		10	11		9			4			17
1	2	3		5	6	7	8		10	11		9			4			18
1	2	3	4	5	6	7†	8	13		11*		10	12		4			19
1	2	3	4		10	7	8			11		9	6		5			20
1	2	3	4	5	6	7	8			11	10	9						21
1	2	3	4	5	10	7	8			11		9			6			22
1	2	3*	4	5	10	7	8	12		11		9			6			23
1	2		4	5	10	7†	8	12		9*		11		6	3	13		24
1	2		4	5	10		8	7		9		11		6	3			25
1	2	12	4	5	10	7	8	13		9		11		6†	3*			26
1	2	3	4	5	10	7*	8	12		11		9		6				27
1	2	3	4	5	10	7	8			11		9		6				28
1	2	3	4	5	6	7	8			9	10	11*		12				29
1	2	3	4	5	6	7	8		10	9		11						30
1	2	3	4	5	6	7	8		10	9		11						31
1		3	4	5	6	7	8	12	10	9		11			2*			32
1	2	3*	4	5	6	7	8		10	9	12	11						33
1	2		4	5	6	7	8		10	9		11			3			34
1	2	3		5	10		8	7		9	12	11*			6			35
1	2		4	5	6	7	8			9		11			3			36
36	34	24	33	35	35	33	36	7	17	35	3	32	4	7	25			
	2							13			4	2	1	1		1	1	
	1	1	6	3	11	5	6	2	7	29		17		1				

39

1983-84

#	Month	Date		Opponent		Score	Scorers	Attendance
1	Aug	20	(a)	Hibernian	W	2-0	MacLeod, Melrose	14,750
2	Sep	3	(h)	Rangers	W	2-1	Aitken, McGarvey	50,662
3		10	(h)	St. Johnstone	W	5-2	Burns 2, McGarvey, Melrose, Morton (og)	11,161
4		17	(a)	Motherwell	W	3-0	Burns, McGarvey, McStay P	14,202
5		24	(a)	Dundee	W	6-2	McClair 4, Burns, Melrose	11,467
6	Oct	1	(h)	St. Mirren	D	1-1	Whittaker	15,289
7		8	(a)	Dundee U	L	1-2	Melrose	20,741
8		15	(h)	Hearts	D	1-1	McGarvey	20,207
9		22	(a)	Aberdeen	L	1-3	Aitken	23,000
10		29	(h)	Hibernian	W	5-1	McClair 2, Provan, Whittaker, MacLeod	13,777
11	Nov	5	(a)	Rangers	W	2-1	McGarvey, Burns	40,000
12		12	(h)	Motherwell	W	4-0	McClair 2, MacLeod, McGarvey	13,408
13		19	(a)	St. Mirren	L	2-4	Burns, Aitken	13,062
14		26	(h)	Dundee	W	1-0	Reid (pen)	14,583
15	Dec	3	(a)	St. Johnstone	W	3-0	Dobbin, Melrose, Aitken	8,131
16		10	(h)	Aberdeen	D	0-0		25,867
17		17	(a)	Hearts	W	3-1	McClair 2, Dobbin	15,298
18		27	(h)	Dundee U	D	1-1	McClair	25,982
19		31	(a)	Hibernian	W	1-0	Blackley (og)	11,234
20	Jan	7	(a)	Motherwell	D	2-2	McGarvey, McStay P	11,268
21	Feb	4	(a)	Aberdeen	L	0-1		22,500
22		11	(h)	St. Johnstone	W	5-2	McClair 2, MacLeod 2, McGarvey	9,439
23		14	(h)	St. Mirren	W	2-0	McGarvey 2	9,835
24		25	(h)	Hearts	W	4-1	McClair 3, Colquhoun	17,950
25	Mar	3	(a)	Dundee U	L	1-3	Aitken	15,326
26		20	(a)	Dundee	L	2-3	Burns, Reid (pen)	7,746
27		31	(h)	Aberdeen	W	1-0	Melrose	19,193
28	Apr	2	(h)	Rangers	W	3-0	McStay P, McStay W, Provan	53,229
29		7	(a)	St. Johnstone	D	0-0		6,667
30		10	(h)	Motherwell	W	4-2	McClair 2, MacLeod, Archdeacon	5,673
31		18	(a)	St. Mirren	W	4-2	McClair 2, Burns, Sinclair	6,122
32		21	(a)	Rangers	L	0-1		40,260
33		24	(h)	Dundee	W	3-0	McClair, Melrose, McAdam	4,956
34		28	(h)	Hibernian	W	3-2	McClair 2, Colquhoun	9,553
35	May	5	(a)	Hearts	D	1-1	Burns	12,281
36		12	(h)	Dundee U	D	1-1	MacLeod	10,281

FINAL LEAGUE POSITION : 2nd in Premier Division

Appearances

Sub. Appearances

Goals

Bonner	McGrain	Reid	Aitken	McAdam	MacLeod	Provan	McStay P	McGarvey	Burns	Melrose	Crainie	Whittaker	McStay W	McClair	Sinclair	Halpin	Latchford	Dobbin	Colquhoun	Archdeacon	Grant	McGugan	
1	2	3	4	5	6	7	8	9*	10	11	12												1
1	2		4		6	7	8	9	10	11*		3	5	12									2
1	2	3	4		6	7*	8	9†	10	11	12		5	13									3
1	2		4	5	6	7	8	9*	10		12	3		11									4
1	2		4	5	6	7†	8		10	9		3*		11	12	13							5
1	2		4	5	6	7	8	9	10	11*		3		12									6
1	2		4	5	10		7	9	11	8		3*		12	6								7
1	2		4	5	6	7	8	9	10	11*				12	3								8
1	2	12	4	5	6*	7	8	9	10					11	3								9
	2*		4	5	6	7	8	9†	10	13		3		11	12		1						10
1	2			5	6	7*	8	9	10	12		3	4	11									11
1	2			5	6		8	9	10			3*	4	7	12	11							12
1	2		4	5	10		8	9	11				6*	7	3	12							13
1	2	3	4		6		8	9	11	10				7	5								14
1	2	3	4		6*		9	11	10				12	7†	5	13		8					15
1	2	3	4	5	6		8	9	10	11				7									16
1	2	3	4	5	10*		8	9						11	6				12	7			17
1	2	3	4	5*	10		8	9						11	6				12	7			18
1	2	3	4		6		8	9					5	11	10				7				19
1	2	3	4		6		8	9†	10	11			5	7*	13				12				20
1	2†	3	4	5	10		8	9	11*	12			13	7	6								21
1	2	3	4	5	10		8	9†	12	13				11	6*				7				22
1	2	3	4	5	10		8	9						11	6				7				23
1	2	3	4	5	6		8	9*	10	12				11					7				24
1			4	5	6		8	9*	10	12		3		11	2				7				25
1	2	3	4	5	6	7	8	9*	10	12				11									26
1	2	3	4	5	10	12	8*		11	9			6	7									27
1	2	3	4	5	10	12	8	13	11*	9†			6	7									28
1	2	3	4	5	10	7	8*		11	9			6	12									29
1	2	3		5*	6	7	8		10†	9			4	11	12				13				30
1	2	3		5		7	8	11	10	9*			4	12	6								31
1	2	3		5	10	12	8	9†	11	1			6	7							4*		32
1		3	4	5	6*		8		10	9			2	11					7		12		33
	2	3	4				8†	13	10	9			12	11			1		7		6	5*	34
			4	5	6		8		10	9		3		11	2		1		7				35
1	2	3	4		6	12	8		10	11			5	9					7*				36
33	33	23	31	28	34	14	34	28	31	20		10	15	28	15	1	3	1	11		2	1	
		1				4		2	1	9	2	3	7	5	3			2	1	1	1		
		2	5	1	7	2	3	10	9	7		2	1	23	1				2	2	1		

41

1984-85

1	Aug	11	(a)	Hibernian	D	0-0		15,500
2		18	(h)	Dundee U	D	1-1	McClair	19,000
3		25	(a)	Rangers	D	0-0		44,000
4	Sep	1	(h)	Morton	W	5-0	McClair 2, McGarvey 2, Grant	12,123
5		8	(a)	Dumbarton	D	1-1	McGarvey	8,416
6		15	(h)	Hearts	W	1-0	McGarvey	18,411
7		22	(a)	St. Mirren	W	2-1	McClair, Colquhoun	12,550
8		27	(a)	Dundee	W	3-2	Burns, Colquhoun, Grant (pen)	13,761
9	Oct	6	(h)	Aberdeen	W	2-1	McGarvey, Provan	31,418
10		13	(h)	Hibernian	W	3-0	Burns, McClair, Grant (pen)	27,863
11		20	(a)	Dundee U	W	3-1	Johnston, MacLeod, Grant	16,738
12	Nov	3	(a)	Morton	L	1-2	Johnston	8,503
13		10	(h)	Dumbarton	W	2-0	Johnston, McGarvey	13,791
14		17	(a)	Hearts	W	5-1	McClair 3, Johnston, Burns	20,117
15		24	(h)	St. Mirren	W	7-1	McGarvey 3, McStay P, Burns, Provan, McClair	16,418
16	Dec	1	(h)	Dundee	W	5-1	Johnston 3, McGarvey, Burns	15,889
17		8	(a)	Aberdeen	L	2-4	Johnston (pen), McGarvey	23,000
18		15	(a)	Hibernian	W	1-0	Johnston	10,000
19		22	(h)	Rangers	D	1-1	McClair	43,748
20		29	(h)	Dundee U	L	1-2	Burns	22,894
21	Jan	1	(a)	Rangers	W	2-1	Johnston, McClair	45,000
22	Feb	2	(a)	St. Mirren	W	2-0	Johnston, Burns	14,025
23		9	(a)	Dundee	L	0-2		12,087
24		19	(h)	Morton	W	4-0	McGarvey, McStay P, Provan, Chalmers	10,197
25		23	(h)	Aberdeen	W	2-0	Johnston, McStay P (pen)	48,824
26	Mar	2	(a)	Dundee U	D	0-0		16,493
27		16	(h)	Hibernian	L	0-1		15,820
28		20	(h)	Hearts	W	3-2	Johnston, MacLeod, McClair	11,522
29		23	(a)	Morton	W	7-2	McClair 4, McGarvey 2, Archdeacon	8,000
30	Apr	3	(a)	Dumbarton	W	2-0	McClair, Johnston	7,000
31		6	(a)	Hearts	W	2-0	McClair, McStay P	14,883
32		20	(h)	St. Mirren	W	3-0	Aitken 2 (2 pens), McGarvey	11,746
33		27	(a)	Aberdeen	D	1-1	Aitken (pen)	23,000
34	May	1	(h)	Rangers	D	1-1	McInally	40,079
35		4	(h)	Dundee	L	0-1		8,815
36		11	(h)	Dumbarton	W	2-0	McClair, McStay W	6,514

FINAL LEAGUE POSITION : 2nd in Premier Division

Appearances

Sub. Appearances

Goals

42

Bonner	Sinclair	Reid	McAdam	McGugan	MacLeod	Colquhoun	Grant	McClair	Burns	McGarvey	McKechnie	McInally A	Aitken	Provan	McGrain	McStay P	McStay W	Johnston	O'Leary	Latchford	Chalmers	Archdeacon	Coyle	No.
1	2	3	4	5	6	7	8	9†	10	11*	12	13												1
1	2	3	5		6†	7*	8	9	10	11		13	4	12										2
1	3		5			7	6	9	10	13		11†	4		2	8*	12							3
1	3		5			6	9	10	11			12	4	7	2	8*								4
1	3*	12	5				6	9†	10	11		13	4	7	2	8								5
1		3	5			7	6	9	10	11*		12	4		2	8								6
1		3	5			7	6	12	10	9	11*		4		2	8								7
1	3*		5		12	7	6	9	10	11			4		2	8								8
1		3	5		10	7*	6	9		11			4	12	2	8								9
1			5	3	6		12	10	11*			4	7	2	8		9							10
1			5	3	6		12	10*	11			4	7	2	8		9							11
1		3	5		10	6	12		11*			4	7	2	8		9							12
1			5	3	12	6	10		11			4	7*	2	8		9							13
1			5	3	6		10	11		12		4	7	2	8		9*							14
1		5*	3	13	6		10	11			4	7†	2	8	12	9								15
1			5	3	6		10	11			4	7	2	8		9								16
1		5*	3	13	6		10	11			4	7	2	8	12†	9								17
1		3	5	6	7*		10		11		4	12	2	8		9								18
1	12	3		6	7†		4	10	11		5	13	2*	8		9								19
1		3		6			4	10	11		5	7	2	8		9								20
1		3		6	7		4	10	11		5		2	8		9								21
1		3	5	4	7			10	11*		12		2	8		9	6							22
1		3	5	4	7			10	11		12		2	8		9*	6							23
				10		4		12	11			5	7	3	8*	2	9†	6	1	13				24
1			5		10	7*			11			4	12	3	8	2	9	6						25
1				10		4	12	11	8			5	7	3		2	9*	6						26
1			5		10	7		11†	12	13		4		3	8	2*	9	6						27
1				6			12	10	11*			4	7	3	8	2	9	5						28
1				6		12		10		11		4	7†	3*	8	2	9	5				13		29
1		3		6			11	10	12			4	7	2	8*		9	5						30
1		3	12	6			11	10				4	7	2*	8		9	5						31
1			5	3	12	6	10	11				4	7*	8	2		9							32
1			5	6	7†	12	10	11				4	13	3	8	2	9*							33
					5	3	12	6	10			11*	4	7		8	2	9	1					34
1				5	3	7†	6	8		10*	11	4			2		9					13	12	35
1			5		6		7		10			4		8	2	9	3					11		36
34	5	15	25	3	30	14	19	25	25	30	1	4	33	19	30	32	11	27	11	2		1		
	1	1	1		1	5	1	7	2	3	1	8			6		3				1	2	1	
					2	2	4	19	7	15		1	3	3		4	1	14			1	1		

43

1985-86

1	Aug	10	(a)	Hearts	D	1-1	McStay P	21,786
2		17	(h)	Motherwell	W	2-1	McClair, Provan	20,189
3		24	(a)	Clydebank	W	2-0	Johnston 2	9,100
4		31	(h)	Rangers	D	1-1	McStay P	28,365
5	Sep	7	(a)	Hibernian	W	5-0	McClair 2, Johnston, Archdeacon, Fulton (og)	13,150
6		14	(h)	Aberdeen	W	2-1	McClair 2	39,450
7		28	(a)	Dundee	W	2-0	McClair, Johnston	15,387
8	Oct	5	(h)	St. Mirren	W	2-0	McClair, McGugan	25,651
9		12	(h)	Hearts	L	0-1		26,683
10		19	(a)	Motherwell	W	2-1	McStay P 2 (1 pen)	13,902
11		26	(h)	Dundee U	L	0-3		25,976
12	Nov	2	(a)	Aberdeen	L	1-4	Provan	23,000
13		9	(a)	Rangers	L	0-3		42,045
14		16	(h)	Clydebank	W	2-0	McGhee 2	14,148
15		23	(h)	Hibernian	D	1-1	Johnston	21,000
16	Dec	14	(a)	Hearts	D	1-1	McGhee	22,163
17		23	(a)	Dundee U	L	0-1		15,074
18		28	(h)	Clydebank	W	2-0	Johnston, McStay P (pen)	13,822
19	Jan	1	(h)	Rangers	W	2-0	McGugan, McClair	49,000
20		4	(a)	Dundee U	L	2-4	McClair 2	16,113
21		11	(h)	Aberdeen	D	1-1	Grant	31,305
22		15	(h)	Motherwell	W	3-2	McGhee, Johnston, McClair	12,002
23		18	(a)	Hibernian	D	2-2	Archdeacon, Burns	13,500
24	Feb	1	(a)	Dundee	W	3-1	Johnston, McStay P, McClair	12,295
25		8	(h)	St. Mirren	D	1-1	Burns	18,102
26		22	(h)	Hearts	D	1-1	Johnston	45,366
27	Mar	15	(h)	Dundee U	D	1-1	MacLeod	22,965
28		22	(a)	Rangers	D	4-4	Johnston, McClair, Burns, MacLeod	41,006
29		29	(a)	Clydebank	W	5-0	McClair 3 (2 pens), Burns, McInally	7,969
30	Apr	2	(h)	Dundee	W	2-1	Johnston, Burns	12,506
31		5	(a)	St. Mirren	W	2-1	MacLeod, McStay P	11,284
32		12	(a)	Aberdeen	W	1-0	Johnston	22,000
33		19	(h)	Hibernian	W	2-0	Archdeacon, McClair	15,966
34		26	(h)	Dundee	W	2-0	McClair, Johnston	14,511
35		30	(a)	Motherwell	W	2-0	McClair 2 (1 pen)	10,545
36	May	3	(a)	St. Mirren	W	5-0	McClair 2, Johnston 2, McStay P	17,557

FINAL LEAGUE POSITION : 1st in Premier League

Appearances

Sub. Appearances

Goals

Bonner	McStay W	Burns	Aitken	McAdam	Grant	Provan	McStay P	Johnston	MacLeod	McClair	McInally	O'Leary	McGrain	McGugan	Archdeacon	Chalmers	McGhee	Coyle	Latchford	Whyte	Shepherd	#
1	2	3	4	5	6	7	8	9	10	11*	12											1
1	2	3	4		6	7	8	9	10	11		5										2
1		3	4	5*	6	7		9	10	8	11	12	2									3
1		3	4	5	6*	7	8	9	10	11	12		2									4
1		3	4		6*		8	9	10	7	11		2	5	12							5
1		3	4		6	7	8	9	10	11			2	5								6
1		3	4		6	7	8	9	10*	11	12		2	5								7
1		3	4		6	7	8*	9	10	11	12		2	5								8
1		3	4		6	7	8	9	10	11			2	5								9
1	12	3	4		6*	7†	8	9	10	11			2	5	13							10
1	12	3	4		6		8	9*	10	7	11†		2	5	13							11
1	2	10	4	5*	6	7	8			9	11†		3	12	13							12
1	2*	3	4	5	10	7	8	13		11†			12	6			9					13
1	2	3	4		6		7	9	10					5	11		8					14
1	2	3	4		6		7	9	10	12				5	11		8*					15
1		3	4		2		8	10	6	7				5	11		9					16
1	12	3	4		2		8	9	6	7†	13			5*	11		10					17
1		10	4		2		7	8	6				3	5	11		9					18
1	2	10	4		6		8			7			3	5	11		9					19
1	2	10	4		6		8			7	12		3		11*		9	5				20
	2		4		6		8	11	10†	7	12	5	3		13		9*		1			21
	2		4		6	12	8	9		7		5	3		11*		10		1			22
	2	11	4		6		8	9		7*		5	3		12		10		1			23
		3	4		6*		8	9	10	7		5	2		11		12		1			24
	12	3	4				8*	9	6	7	13	5	2		11		10†		1			25
	2	11	4					9	6	7			3	5			8*		1	10	12	26
1	2	10	4		6		8	9	12	7†		5*			11		13			3		27
1	2	10	4		12		8†	9	6	7	13	5			11*					3		28
1		10	4				8	9	6	7	12	5	2		11*					3		29
1		10	4				8	9	6	7	12	5	2		11*					3		30
1		10	4		13		8		6	7	9†	5	2	12	11*					3		31
1		11	4		6		8	9	10	7		5*	2		12					3		32
1		10	4				8*	9	6	7			2	5	11		12			3		33
1		10	4		12		8	9	6	7			2*	5	11		13		3†	3		34
1		10	4				8	9	6	7			2	5	11*		12			3		35
1		10	4		12		8	9	6	7			2*	5	11					3		36
30	14	34	36	5	26	11	34	31	29	33	5	12	27	19	19		13	1	6	11		
	4				4	1		1	1	1	11	1	1	2	4	3	5			1		
		5		1	2	8	15	3	22	1			2	3			4					

45

1986-87

1	Aug	9	(h)	Dundee	W	1-0	Johnston	35,433
2		13	(a)	Motherwell	W	4-0	Johnston 2, McClair 2 (1 pen)	13,325
3		16	(a)	Clydebank	W	1-0	Johnston	9,850
4		23	(h)	Aberdeen	D	1-1	MacLeod	46,073
5		31	(a)	Rangers	L	0-1		43,502
6	Sep	6	(h)	Hamilton A	W	4-1	McInally 3, Johnston	17,036
7		13	(a)	Dundee U	D	2-2	McClair, McStay P	19,792
8		20	(h)	Hibernian	W	5-1	McClair 2, McStay P, Johnston, McInally	22,140
9		27	(a)	Falkirk	W	1-0	Johnston	16,400
10	Oct	4	(h)	St. Mirren	W	2-0	Johnston, McClair	20,258
11		8	(h)	Hearts	W	2-0	Johnston, McClair (pen)	34,382
12		11	(a)	Dundee	W	3-0	Johnston 2, McClair	13,351
13		18	(h)	Motherwell	W	3-1	McInally 2, Shepherd	19,395
14		29	(h)	Clydebank	W	6-0	McInally 2, McClair 2, McGhee, MacLeod	10,161
15	Nov	1	(h)	Rangers	D	1-1	McClair	60,000
16		8	(a)	Hamilton A	W	2-1	Johnston, McClair (pen)	10,000
17		15	(h)	Dundee U	W	1-0	Johnston	34,390
18		19	(a)	Hibernian	W	1-0	McClair	17,800
19		22	(h)	Falkirk	W	4-2	Johnston 2, McInally, Grant	16,545
20		26	(a)	Aberdeen	D	1-1	McClair (pen)	22,040
21		29	(a)	St. Mirren	W	1-0	O'Leary	16,233
22	Dec	3	(a)	Hearts	L	0-1		25,886
23		6	(h)	Dundee	W	2-1	Johnston 2	19,300
24		13	(a)	Motherwell	D	1-1	McClair	11,760
25		20	(h)	Aberdeen	D	1-1	McInally	35,624
26		27	(a)	Clydebank	D	1-1	McClair	8,367
27	Jan	1	(a)	Rangers	L	0-2		43,206
28		3	(h)	Hamilton A	W	8-3	McClair 4, McInally 2, MacLeod 2	16,380
29		10	(a)	Dundee U	L	2-3	McClair 2	18,576
30		21	(h)	Hibernian	W	1-0	Rogan	21,583
31		24	(a)	Falkirk	W	2-1	Johnston 2	15,500
32	Feb	7	(h)	St. Mirren	W	3-0	Johnston 2, McClair	20,143
33		14	(h)	Hearts	D	1-1	McClair	38,198
34		28	(a)	Dundee	L	1-4	McClair	12,455
35	Mar	7	(h)	Motherwell	W	3-1	Shepherd, Aitken, McAdam (og)	14,840
36		14	(a)	Aberdeen	L	0-1		20,000
37		21	(h)	Clydebank	W	3-0	McClair 2 (1 pen), McInally	13,029
38		28	(a)	Hamilton A	W	3-2	McClair, McInally, Archdeacon	8,505
39	Apr	4	(h)	Rangers	W	3-1	McClair 2 (2 pens), Archdeacon	60,800
40		11	(a)	Hibernian	W	4-1	McClair, Johnston, McInally, McStay P	14,000
41		18	(h)	Dundee U	D	1-1	McClair	30,798
42		25	(a)	St. Mirren	W	3-1	McClair 2, Johnston	11,680
43	May	2	(h)	Falkirk	L	1-2	McClair (pen)	14,238
44		9	(a)	Hearts	L	0-1		12,596

FINAL LEAGUE POSITION : 2nd in Premier Division

Appearances

Sub. Appearances

Goals

Bonner	McStay W	Whyte	Aitken	McGugan	MacLeod	McClair	McStay P	Johnston	Burns	Archdeacon	McInally	Grant	McGrain	O'Leary	Smith	Shepherd	McGhee M	Latchford	McGuire	Rogan	No.
1	2	3	4	5	6	7	8	9	10	11*	12										1
1	2	3	4	5	6	7	8	9	10	11											2
1	2†	3	4	5	6	7	8	9	10	11*	13	12									3
1	2*	3	4	5	10	7	8	9	11	12			6								4
1	12	3	4	5	6	7	8	9	10*	11†	13	2									5
1	2		4		10	12	8	9*		13	11	6	3	5	7†						6
1	2	3	4	5	10	7	8	9			12	6				11*					7
1	2*	5	4		6	7	8	9	10	11†	13			12	5						8
1	2*	5	4		6	7†	8	9	3		11			12		10	13				9
1	2*	5	4		6	7	8	9	3		11			12		10					10
1	2*	5	4		6	7	8	9†	3	13	11			12		10					11
1	2*	5	4		6	7	8	9	3		11			12		10†	13				12
1		5	4		6*	7	8	9	3		11	2				10	12				13
	2	5	4		10*	7	8†			13	11	6	3	12			9	1			14
1		5	4	3		7	8*	9			12	6	2			10	11				15
1		3	4		10	7	8	9			13	6	2*	5		12	11†				16
1		3	4		6	7	8	9			11	2		5		10*	12				17
1		3	4		6	7	8	9			11	2	12	5		10*					18
1		3	4		6†	7	8	9			11	2		5		10*	13		12		19
1		3	4			7	8	9		13	11	2	12	5		6	10†				20
1		3	4			7	8	9		12	11	6	2	5		10*					21
1		3	4			7	8	9		13	11*	6	2	5		10†	12				22
1		3	4	5*		7	8	9		11	10†	2	6	12			13				23
1		3	4	5		7	8	9		11*	10	2	6	12							24
1		3	2	5	4	7	8	9		13	10	6*		12			11†				25
1	2*	3	4	5	10	7	8	9		13	11†	6				12					26
1		3	4	5	6	7	8	9		11†	10*	2		12			13				27
1	6	5			10	7	8		11	9	4	2								3	28
1	6	5†			10	7	8	9*		13	4	2				11	12			3	29
1			4		6	7	8	9			11	2	12	5		10*				3	30
1		5	4		10	7	8	9		11*	12	6	2							3	31
1		5	4	12	10†	7	8	9		13	11	6	2*							3	32
1		5	4		10	7	8	9		11		6	2*	12						3	33
1		5	4		10	7	8	9			12	6	2				3*	11			34
1	6	4	5			7	8	9		11*	12	2				10				3	35
1	6	4	5	12		7	8	9		11*	13	2				10†				3	36
1	6	4	5†		10	7	8	9		11*	13	2		12						3	37
1	6	4	5		10	7	8	9		11*	12	2								3	38
1	6	4	5		10	7	8	9		11*	12	2								3	39
1	6	4	5		10	7	8	9		11*	12	2								3	40
1	6	4	5		10	7	8	9		13	12	2					11†			3*	41
1	6*	4	5		10	7†	8	9		11	12	2					13			3	42
1	6	4	5*		10	7	8	9		11†	12	2					13			3	43
1	6	4	5		10*	7	8	9		11	12	2								3	44
43	15	42	42	21	37	43	43	39	14	12	29	32	21	15	3	16	6	1		10	
	1			1	1	1		1	3	17	9	5	5	1	3	5	11				
			1		4	35	3	23		2	15	1		1		2	1			1	

47

1987-88

1	Aug	8	(a)	Morton	W	4-0	Walker 2, McGhee, Stark	15,500
2		12	(h)	Hearts	W	1-0	McGhee	29,815
3		15	(h)	Motherwell	W	4-0	Walker 2, McGhee, Stark	24,478
4		22	(a)	Dunfermline A	L	1-2	Walker (pen)	18,070
5		29	(h)	Rangers	W	1-0	Stark	60,800
6	Sep	5	(a)	Dundee U	D	0-0		16,192
7		12	(a)	Falkirk	W	1-0	Burns	17,500
8		19	(h)	Aberdeen	D	2-2	Burns, Stark	38,944
9		26	(a)	St. Mirren	W	1-0	Whyte	18,011
10	Oct	3	(h)	Hibernian	D	1-1	Walker	31,805
11		7	(a)	Dundee	D	1-1	Walker (pen)	13,238
12		10	(h)	Morton	W	3-1	Walker, Whyte, McAvennie	22,780
13		17	(a)	Rangers	D	2-2	Walker, Butcher (og)	44,000
14		24	(h)	Dundee U	L	1-2	Shepherd	31,032
15		28	(h)	Falkirk	W	3-2	Stark 2, Archdeacon	11,381
16		31	(a)	Aberdeen	W	1-0	McAvennie	21,000
17	Nov	7	(a)	Hearts	D	1-1	McGhee	29,000
18		14	(h)	Dundee	W	5-0	Walker 2, McAvennie 2, Miller	31,664
19		17	(a)	Motherwell	W	2-0	Walker, Whyte	17,261
20		21	(h)	Dunfermline A	W	4-0	Walker 2 (2 pens), McAvennie, Stark	28,534
21		25	(h)	St. Mirren	W	1-0	Grant	26,718
22		28	(a)	Hibernian	W	1-0	McAvennie	23,500
23	Dec	5	(a)	Morton	W	4-0	McAvennie 4	16,500
24		12	(h)	Hearts	D	2-2	Walker (pen), McStay	43,968
25		19	(h)	Aberdeen	D	0-0		37,721
26		22	(a)	Falkirk	W	2-0	Walker, McStay	12,000
27		26	(a)	Dundee U	W	2-1	Walker (pen), Miller	18,458
28	Jan	2	(h)	Rangers	W	2-0	McAvennie 2	60,800
29		9	(a)	St. Mirren	D	1-1	Money (og)	19,300
30		16	(h)	Hibernian	W	2-0	McStay, Miller	34,896
31	Feb	6	(h)	Motherwell	W	1-0	Walker	25,035
32		13	(a)	Dundee	W	2-1	McAvennie, Morris	17,106
33		27	(h)	Morton	W	1-0	Aitken (pen)	23,120
34	Mar	2	(a)	Dunfermline A	W	4-0	McAvennie 2, Walker, Stark	17,448
35		5	(h)	Falkirk	W	2-0	McGhee, Walker	23,174
36		20	(a)	Rangers	W	2-1	McStay, Walker	43,650
37		26	(h)	Dundee U	D	0-0		34,933
38		30	(a)	Aberdeen	W	1-0	Walker	22,700
39	Apr	2	(a)	Hibernian	W	2-0	Walker, Grant	19,500
40		5	(h)	St. Mirren	W	2-0	Walker, McStay	45,465
41		16	(a)	Hearts	L	1-2	McGhee	26,200
42		23	(h)	Dundee	W	3-0	Walker 2, Morris	72,000
43		30	(a)	Motherwell	W	1-0	Rogan	13,874
44	May	7	(h)	Dunfermline A	W	1-0	Morris	44,482

FINAL LEAGUE POSITION : 1st in Premier Division

Appearances

Sub. Appearances

Goals

Bonner	Morris	Rogan	Aitken	Whyte	Grant	Stark	McStay P	McGhee	Walker	Burns	Archdeacon	McGugan	Shepherd	McGuire	McKnight	McCarthy	McAvennie	McCarrison	Miller	Baillie	
1	2	3	4	5	6	7	8	9	10	11*	12										1
1	2	3	4	5	6	7	8	9	10	11											2
1	2	3	4	5		7*	8†	9	10	11	6	12	13								3
1	2	3	4	5*	6	7	8	9	10	11†	13	12									4
	2	3	4	5	6	7	8	9	10	11					1						5
	2	3	4	5	6	7	8	9	10	11					1						6
	2	3	4	5	6	7	8	9	10	11					1						7
	2	3	4	5	6	7	8	9*	10	11	12				1						8
	2	3	4	5	6	7	8		10	11	9*	12			1						9
	2	3	4	5	11	7	8		10		12				1	6*	9				10
	2	3	4	5	11†	7*	8		10		13	12			1	6	9				11
	2		4	3	6	7	8		10	11					1	5	9				12
	2	12	4	3*	6	7	8		10	11†	13				1	5	9				13
1	2		4	3	6	7*	8		10	11	12					5		9			14
1	2		4	3	6	7*	8	12	10†	11	13					5	9				15
1	2		4	3	6	7	8	11	10							5	9				16
1	2	12	4	3	6*	7	8	11	10		13					5	9†				17
1	2	3	4	5	6		8		10	11							9		7		18
1	2	13	4	3	6		8	12	10*	11†						5	9		7		19
1	2		4	3	6	11	8		10							5	9		7		20
1	2		4	3	6	11	8		10							5	9		7		21
1	2	12	4	3	6	11*	8		10							5	9		7		22
1	2		4	3	6	11	8		10							5	9		7		23
1	2	13	4	3†	6	11	8	12	10							5	9		7*		24
1	2	3	4	5	6	11	8	12	10*								9		7		25
1	2	3	4	5†	6	11	8	12	10								9*		7	13	26
	2	3	4		6*	11	8		10		12				1		9		7	5	27
	2	3	4		6	11	8		10						1		9		7	5	28
	2	3	4		6		8		10	11					1		9		7	5	29
1	2		4	3	6		8		10	11							9		7	5	30
1	2		4	3	6		8		10	11						5	9		7		31
1	2	3	4		11		8	12	10*							5	9		7	6	32
1	2		4	3	6	7*	8		10	11						5	9		12		33
1	2		4	3	6	11*	8	13	10†	12						5	9		7		34
1	2	13	4	3	6	11	8†	9	10	12						5			7*		35
1	2	12	4	3		7	8		10	6							9		11*	5	36
1	2	13	4	3	6	7*	8		10	11†							9		12	5	37
1	2	3	4		6	7	8		10								9		11	5	38
1	2	3	4		6	7	8	12	10								9		11*	5	39
1	2	3	4		6*	7†	8	9	10		13	12							11	5	40
1	2	3	4	5		7*	8	11	10	6							9†		13	12	41
1	2	3	4		6	12	8	13	10	11						5	9†		7*		42
1	2	3				7	8	12	10*	6	13					5	9		11†	4	43
1	2	3	4	6	13	7†	8*		10		12					5	9		11		44
32	44	25	43	41	36	34	44	15	42	21	4	1			12	22	32	1	24	11	
	8			1	3			9	6	6	1	6	1						3	2	
	3	1	1	3	2	8	5	6	26	2	1		1				15		3		

1988-89

1	Aug	13	(h)	Hearts	W	1-0	McAvennie	46,845
2		20	(a)	Dundee U	L	0-1		18,769
3		27	(a)	Rangers	L	1-5	McAvennie	42,858
4	Sep	3	(h)	Hamilton A	W	2-1	McAvennie, Miller	24,084
5		17	(h)	Aberdeen	L	1-3	Miller (pen)	37,769
6		24	(a)	Dundee	L	0-1		15,515
7		28	(h)	Motherwell	W	3-1	McAvennie 2, Walker	20,187
8	Oct	1	(a)	Hibernian	L	1-3	Walker	24,000
9		8	(h)	St. Mirren	W	7-1	McGhee 3, Stark 2, McStay, Miller	26,091
10		12	(h)	Dundee U	W	1-0	Miller	36,760
11		22	(a)	Hearts	W	2-0	McGhee, McAvennie	24,017
12		29	(h)	Dundee	L	2-3	Stark, Morris	23,843
13	Nov	2	(a)	Aberdeen	D	2-2	Stark 2	22,000
14		5	(a)	Hamilton A	W	8-0	McGhee 3, McAvennie 3 (1 pen), Miller, Stark	10,500
15		12	(h)	Rangers	W	3-1	McGhee, Stark, Butcher (og)	60,113
16		19	(h)	Hibernian	W	1-0	McAvennie	35,251
17		26	(a)	St. Mirren	W	3-2	Burns 2, McAvennie	21,266
18	Dec	3	(a)	Motherwell	W	3-1	McGhee, McAvennie, McStay	16,392
19		10	(h)	Aberdeen	D	0-0		42,437
20		17	(a)	Dundee U	L	0-1		18,745
21		31	(h)	Hearts	W	4-2	McGhee 2, Stark 2	44,646
22	Jan	3	(a)	Rangers	L	1-4	Morris	42,515
23		7	(h)	Hamilton A	W	2-0	Walker, Miller	18,679
24		14	(h)	St. Mirren	W	2-1	Walker (pen), Morris	26,796
25		21	(a)	Hibernian	W	3-1	Walker, McGhee, McStay	23,500
26	Feb	11	(h)	Motherwell	L	1-2	Walker	21,445
27		25	(a)	Dundee	W	3-0	Walker, McStay, McCarrison	14,559
28	Mar	11	(a)	Hearts	W	1-0	McGhee	23,087
29		25	(h)	Dundee U	W	1-0	McGhee	32,589
30	Apr	1	(h)	Rangers	L	1-2	Walker	60,800
31		8	(a)	Hamilton A	L	0-2		9,301
32		12	(a)	Motherwell	D	2-2	McGhee, McStay	10,507
33		22	(h)	Dundee	W	2-1	McGhee, Rogan	16,000
34		29	(h)	Aberdeen	D	0-0		21,500
35	May	6	(h)	Hibernian	W	1-0	Miller	18,316
36		13	(a)	St. Mirren	W	1-0	Miller	13,057

FINAL LEAGUE POSITION : 3rd in Premier Division

Appearances

Sub. Appearances

Goals

#	Andrews	Morris	Rogan	Whyte	McCarthy	Grant	Miller	McStay P	McAvennie	Walker	Burns	Aitken	McGhee	Stark	Archdeacon	Rough	Baillie	Traynor	Fulton	Bonner	Elliot D	Mathie	McCahill	McCarrison	Coyne	#
1	1	2	3	4	5	6	7	8	9	10	11															1
2	1	2	3	6	5*	7	13	8	9	10	12	4	11†													2
3	1	2	3	12	5	6	13	8	9	10	11*	4		7†												3
4	1	2	3		5	6	7*	8	9	10	11	4			12											4
5	1	2	3	6*	5		7	8	9	10†	11	4		12	13											5
6		2	3	6			7*	8	9	10	11	4	13	12		1	5†									6
7		2	3					8	9	10	11	4		7		1	5	6								7
8		2	3	13			12	8	9	10	11†	4		7*		1	5	6								8
9		2	3	6	5†		11*	8	9			4	10	7	12	1			13							9
10		2	3	6	5		11	8	9			4	10	7		1										10
11		2	3	6	5				9	10	11	4	8	7						1						11
12		2	3	5*			11	8	9		6	4	10	7†	13		12			1						12
13		2	3	6	5			8	9		11	4	10	7						1						13
14		2	3	6	5		12	8	9*		11†	4	10	7	13					1						14
15		2	3	6	5			8	9		11	4	10	7						1						15
16		2	3	6	5			8	9		11	4	10	7						1						16
17		2	3	6	5			8	9		11	4	10	7						1						17
18		2	3	6	5			8	9		11	4	10	7	12					1						18
19		2	3*	6				8	9		11	4	10	7			5			1						19
20		2	3	6		7†	12	8	9	13	11*	4	10				5			1						20
21		2	3	6	5	12		8*	9		11	4	10	7						1						21
22		2	3		5			8	9*	12	11	4	10	7†	13			6		1						22
23		2	3		5	6		8	9		11	4	10	7*						1	12					23
24		2	3		5	6	7	8*	9		11	4	10					12		1						24
25		2	3	4	5	6	7	8	9		11		10							1						25
26		2	3		5	6		8	9	7	11		10†	12			4*			1		13				26
27		2	3		5	6		8	9†		11	4	10	7*						1			12	13		27
28		2			5	6		8	9	3		4	10	7						1			11			28
29		2	3			6		8	10*		11	4	9	7						1		5			12	29
30		2	3			6	13	8	9*		11	4	10	7†						1		5			12	30
31		2	3			6	7	8	9*					12			5		11	1		4			10	31
32						6	11*	8		12	3	4	9	7				2	13	1		5†			10	32
33			3	5	2	11		8			6	4	10	7						1					9	33
34			3	5	2	11		8	9*		6	4	10	7						1			12			34
35		2	3	6	5	7	9	8				4	10							1			11			35
36		2†	3	6	5	7	9	8			13	4	10*							1			11		12	36
	5	33	34	20	26	20	16	33	23	19	30	32	28	22	2	5	8	3	1	26	2		4		4	
		2		1		6		3	2			1	3	8	1	1	2		2		1	1		1	3	
		3	1		1		8	5	12		8	2	16	9											1	

51

1989-90

1	Aug	12	(a)	Hearts	W	3-1	Coyne 3 (1 pen)	25,932
2		19	(h)	Dunfermline A	W	1-0	Galloway	34,000
3		26	(h)	Rangers	D	1-1	Dziekanowski	54,000
4	Sep	9	(a)	St. Mirren	L	0-1		19,813
5		16	(a)	Dundee U	D	2-2	Morris, Coyne	16,624
6		23	(h)	Motherwell	D	1-1	McStay	29,000
7		30	(a)	Aberdeen	D	1-1	Miller	21,374
8	Oct	4	(h)	Hibernian	W	3-1	Walker 2, Dziekanowski	36,000
9		14	(a)	Dundee	W	3-1	Aitken, Coyne, Dziekanowski	16,215
10		21	(h)	Hearts	W	2-1	Aitken, Coyne	38,105
11		28	(a)	Dunfermline A	L	0-2		19,588
12	Nov	4	(a)	Rangers	L	0-1		41,598
13		18	(h)	Dundee U	L	0-1		32,350
14		22	(h)	St. Mirren	D	1-1	Miller	23,100
15		25	(a)	Motherwell	D	0-0		16,029
16	Dec	2	(h)	Aberdeen	W	1-0	Walker (pen)	38,300
17		9	(a)	Hibernian	W	3-0	Dziekanowski, Walker, Wdowczyk	18,000
18		16	(h)	Dundee	W	4-1	Dziekanowski, Walker, Miller, McStay	17,860
19		26	(a)	Hearts	D	0-0		23,259
20		30	(h)	Dunfermline A	L	0-2		30,548
21	Jan	2	(h)	Rangers	L	0-1		54,000
22		6	(a)	St. Mirren	W	2-0	Dziekanowski, Miller	14,813
23		13	(a)	Dundee U	L	0-2		16,635
24		27	(h)	Motherwell	L	0-1		23,000
25	Feb	3	(a)	Dundee	D	0-0		14,100
26		10	(h)	Hibernian	D	1-1	Dziekanowski	25,000
27		17	(a)	Aberdeen	D	1-1	McStay	22,100
28	Mar	3	(h)	Dundee U	W	3-0	Galloway, Whyte, Miller	23,541
29		10	(h)	Hearts	D	1-1	Coyne	34,792
30		24	(a)	Dunfermline A	D	0-0		14,044
31	Apr	1	(a)	Rangers	L	0-3		41,926
32		7	(h)	St. Mirren	L	0-3		18,481
33		17	(a)	Hibernian	L	0-1		11,000
34		21	(h)	Dundee	D	1-1	Creaney	15,115
35		28	(a)	Motherwell	D	1-1	Dziekanowski	10,322
36	May	2	(h)	Aberdeen	L	1-3	Walker	20,154

FINAL LEAGUE POSITION : 5th in Premier Division

Appearances

Sub. Appearances

Goals

Bonner	Morris	Burns	Aitken	Whyte	Grant	Galloway	McStay	Dziekanowski	Coyne	Fulton	Walker	Hewitt	Rogan	McCahill	Elliott P	Miller	Mathie	Wdowczyk	Elliot D	Creaney	Stark								
1	2	3	4	5	6	7	8	9*	10	11	12																		1
1	2	3	4	5	6	7	8	9	10			11																	2
1	2	3	4	5	6	7	8	9	10			11																	3
1	2	3*	4	5	6	7	8	9	10		13	11†	12																4
1	2		4	5		7	8	9*	10	11	12		3	6															5
1	2				4	6	7	8	9	10*	11	12			3														6
1	2			4	6	7	8	9	12		10*				3	5	11												7
1	2			4	6	7	8	9			10				3	5	11												8
1	2	12		4	6		7	8*	9	13	10†				3	5	11												9
1	2	3		4	6		7	8	9	13	10†					5	12	11*											10
1	2	3		4	6		7	8	9	10	12					5	11*												11
1	2	3		4	6		7	8	9*	10	12					5	11												12
1	2	3			12	7	8	9		6†	10*	13	4		5	11													13
1	2				6	7	12	8	9		10	13	3		5	11†		4*											14
1	2				6	7	12	8	9		10	13	3†		5	11*		4											15
1	2			4	6	7	12	8	9		10*	11			5			3											16
1	2			4	6	8	7		9		10	11			5			3											17
1	2			4	6	7	12	8	9		10	11†	5*			13		3											18
1	2			4	6	12	7*	8	9†	13	10	11			5			3											19
1	2			4	6	7†		8	9	13	10*	11			5	12		3											20
1	2			4	6	7	10†	8	12	9	13				5	11*		3											21
1				4	6	2	8	9†		10	12	13			5	11	7*	3											22
1	2				6	4	8	9		10	12				5	11	7*	3											23
1	2				6	4	8	9	13	11	10†			5		7*		3	12										24
1	2			6	7*	4	8	9	10†	12	13				11	5		3											25
1	2			6	7	4*	8	9	10†	11	13				5	12		3											26
1	2			6	7	4	8	9	10	11*					5	12		3											27
1	2			6	7	4	8	9	10						5	11		3											28
1	2			6	7	4	8	9*	10		12				5	11		3											29
1	2			6	7		8		10*	12	9		4†	5		13		3		11									30
1				6	2	7	8	9†	10	12	13		4*	5		11		3											31
1	2			6	7	4	8		10		9*			5		11†		3	12	13									32
1	2			6	7†	4*	8	13		11	10			5		12		3	9										33
1	2			6	4		8			11*	10		12		5	9†	7	3	13										34
1				6	4	2	8	9*		11	10†			5		12		3	13	7									35
1				6	4	2	8	9		11*	10			5		12		3	13	7†									36
36	32		18	35	24	29	35	31	17	13	19	8		2	25	16	5		2	2									
			2	4		2	6	3	13	4					1			2	4										
	1		2	1		2	3	8	7		6				5		1		1										

1990-91

1	Aug	25	(a)	Motherwell	L	0-2		17,652
2	Sep	1	(h)	Aberdeen	L	0-3		45,222
3		8	(h)	Hibernian	W	2-0	Miller, Dziekanowski	28,068
4		15	(a)	Rangers	D	1-1	Whyte	38,543
5		22	(h)	Hearts	W	3-0	Miller 2, Creaney	38,409
6		29	(a)	St. Mirren	W	3-2	Creaney 2, McStay	20,097
7	Oct	6	(h)	St. Johnstone	D	0-0		27,014
8		13	(a)	Dunfermline A	D	1-1	McStay	16,063
9		20	(h)	Dundee U	D	0-0		34,363
10	Nov	3	(a)	Aberdeen	L	0-3		21,500
11		6	(h)	Motherwell	W	2-1	Coyne 2	20,317
12		10	(a)	Hearts	L	0-1		19,189
13		17	(h)	St. Mirren	W	4-1	Baillie, Miller, Creaney, Coyne	25,686
14		25	(h)	Rangers	L	1-2	Elliott	52,265
15	Dec	1	(a)	Hibernian	W	3-0	Coyne 2, Nicholas	16,219
16		8	(a)	Dundee U	L	1-3	Coyne	16,895
17		15	(h)	Dunfermline A	L	1-2	Nicholas	18,875
18		22	(a)	St. Johnstone	L	2-3	Coyne, Nicholas	10,260
19		29	(h)	Hearts	D	1-1	Coyne	28,118
20	Jan	2	(a)	Rangers	L	0-2		38,398
21		5	(h)	Hibernian	D	1-1	Coyne	20,521
22		19	(h)	Aberdeen	W	1-0	Coyne	28,187
23		30	(a)	Motherwell	D	1-1	Dziekanowski	13,542
24	Feb	2	(h)	Dundee U	W	1-0	Coyne	26,172
25	Mar	2	(h)	St. Johnstone	W	3-0	Coyne, Elliott, Miller	24,560
26		6	(a)	Dunfermline A	W	1-0	Creaney	12,458
27		9	(a)	Hibernian	W	2-0	Miller 2	11,500
28		12	(a)	St. Mirren	W	2-0	Creaney 2	11,268
29		24	(h)	Rangers	W	3-0	Rogan, Miller, Coyne	52,000
30		30	(h)	Motherwell	L	1-2	Coyne	21,252
31	Apr	6	(a)	Aberdeen	L	0-1		22,500
32		13	(a)	Dundee U	L	1-2	Malpas (og)	12,603
33		20	(h)	Dunfermline A	W	5-1	Coyne 2, Nicholas 2, Whyte	14,268
34		27	(a)	Hearts	W	1-0	Nicholas	17,085
35	May	5	(h)	St. Mirren	W	1-0	Coyne	17,200
36		11	(a)	St. Johnstone	W	3-2	Nicholas, Galloway, Coyne (pen)	9,486

FINAL LEAGUE POSITION : 3rd in Premier Division

Appearances

Sub. Appearances

Goals

Bonner	Morris	Wdowczyk	Grant	Elliott P	Whyte	Hayes	McStay	Dziekanowski	Walker	Collins	McLaughlin	Miller	Nicholas	Baillie	Fulton	McCarrison	Creaney	Rogan	Galloway	Hewitt	McNally	Coyne	Britton	Mathie	#
1	2	3	4	5	6	7†	8	9	10*	11	12	13											.		1
1	2		4	5	6†	7	8	9	12	11	3	13	10*												2
1		2	5				8	9*	10	11	3	7†		4	6		12	13							3
1	2		4		6		8	9*	10	11		7		5			12	3							4
1		2	5	6		8	9	10†	11		7			4*			13	3	12						5
1		2	5	6		8	9*		11		7			4			10	3			12				6
1	2		8	5	6*		9		11		7			4			10	3			12				7
1		3	2	5		8	9		11		7*			4			10	6			12				8
1	12	3	2	5		13	8		11		7†			4*			10	6				9			9
1		3	2	5		12	8	9*	11		13			4†			10	6	7						10
1		3				8			11		7		5	4			10	6			2	9			11
1		3	2			8	12		11		7		5	4†			10*	6	13			9			12
1		3	8†				11	7*	9	5	4		10	6			13				2	12			13
1		3*	8	5			11	7†	9	6	4		10	12							2	13			14
1		3	8	5			11*		9	4			10	6	12						2	7			15
1		3	12	5		8			11		9	4*		10†	6						2	7	13		16
1		3	2	5	6	8			11		7*	12		10				4				9			17
1	13	3†	2	5		8	12		11		9*	6	4								10		7		18
1	2	3	4	5		8	12		11		9†			13	6						10		7*		19
1	2		4	5	6		8	10*	11		13	12		7†	3					9					20
1	2		4	5	6		8		11		12			10	7*	3					9				21
1	2			5	6		8	13	11		7			12	10†	3*		4			9				22
1	2	3		5	6		8	10	12	11		7*								4	9				23
1		3	4	5	6	12	8	10*	11		7									2	9				24
1	4			5	6		8			11		7					10*	3			2	9		12	25
1	4			5	6		8			11		7					10	3			2	9			26
1	4	12	5		6	13	8			11		7					10†	3			2*	9			27
1	2	5	4		6	7*	8			11		12					10	3				9			28
1		2		5	6		8	13	11*	7				12			10†	3			4	9			29
1	4		8	5	6			10†	11		7*						12	3			2	9	13		30
1	2*	4		5	6		8	13	11		7						10	3			12	9†			31
1		3	4	5	6		8		11*		7†	10					13	12			2	9			32
1		2	4*	5	6		8		11		7†	10						3			12	9		13	33
1	12	3			6		8		11		7*	10†	4				13	5			2	9			34
1		5	4		6		8		11		7	10†	12	3			13				2*	9			35
1		3	4		6					11		7*	10	5	11		12		8		2	9			36
36	15	23	27	27	24	3	30	11	6	35	2	24	12	8	19		22	25	3	1	17	24		2	
	3	1	1			4		3	5		1		6	2	1		2	1	9	2	4	3	2	2	
			2	2		2	2	1		8	6	1		7	1	1					18				

55

1991-92

1	Aug	10	(a)	Dundee U	W	4-3	Nicholas, Coyne, Collins 2	16,535
2		13	(a)	Dunfermline A	W	3-1	Nicholas 2, Coyne	13,264
3		17	(h)	Falkirk	W	4-1	Gillespie, Coyne 2, Collins	32,459
4		24	(a)	Aberdeen	L	0-1		21,800
5		31	(h)	Rangers	L	0-2		51,382
6	Sep	7	(h)	St. Mirren	D	0-0		21,323
7		14	(a)	St. Johnstone	L	0-1		9,993
8		21	(h)	Airdrie	W	3-1	Miller, Galloway, Nicholas (pen)	17,552
9		28	(a)	Hibernian	D	1-1	Nicholas	19,000
10	Oct	5	(h)	Hearts	W	3-1	McNally, Nicholas (pen), Cascarino	33,106
11		8	(a)	Motherwell	W	2-0	Coyne, Nicholas	13,283
12		12	(h)	Dundee U	W	4-1	Nicholas 2, Coyne, Galloway	27,845
13		19	(a)	Falkirk	L	3-4	Collins, McStay 2	11,600
14		26	(a)	St. Mirren	W	5-0	McStay, Coyne 2, Creaney, O'Neill	10,442
15		30	(h)	St. Johnstone	W	4-0	Nicholas 2 (1 pen), Collins, Coyne	18,620
16	Nov	2	(a)	Rangers	D	1-1	Cascarino	37,387
17		9	(h)	Aberdeen	W	2-1	Nicholas, Creaney	36,837
18		16	(a)	Hearts	L	1-3	Coyne	22,666
19		20	(h)	Motherwell	D	2-2	Nicholas 2	16,215
20		23	(a)	Airdrie	W	3-0	Cascarino, Coyne, Creaney	10,102
21		30	(h)	Dunfermline A	W	1-0	Coyne	20,452
22	Dec	4	(h)	Hibernian	D	0-0		22,077
23		7	(a)	Dundee U	D	1-1	Morris	11,145
24		14	(h)	St. Mirren	W	4-0	Collins, Creaney 2, Lambert (og)	16,831
25		28	(a)	Aberdeen	D	2-2	Mowbray, Cascarino	20,422
26	Jan	1	(h)	Rangers	L	1-3	Mowbray	51,383
27		4	(h)	Hearts	L	1-2	Collins	30,415
28		8	(a)	St. Johnstone	W	4-2	McStay, Gillespie, Coyne, Collins	9,283
29		11	(a)	Motherwell	D	0-0		12,115
30		18	(a)	Dunfermline A	W	1-0	Coyne	9,863
31	Feb	1	(h)	Falkirk	W	2-0	Coyne, McStay	16,929
32		8	(h)	Airdrie	W	2-0	Creaney 2	18,845
33		22	(a)	Hibernian	W	2-0	Creaney, Nicholas	16,163
34		29	(a)	Hearts	W	2-1	Creaney 2	20,863
35	Mar	14	(h)	Aberdeen	W	1-0	Collins	29,202
36		17	(h)	Motherwell	W	4-1	Nicholas, McStay, Creaney, Miller	15,521
37		21	(a)	Rangers	W	2-0	Nicholas, Creaney	42,160
38		28	(h)	Dundee U	W	3-1	Creaney, Nicholas, Whyte	22,522
39	Apr	4	(a)	Falkirk	W	3-0	Creaney, Nicholas, Collins	8,842
40		8	(a)	St. Mirren	D	1-1	Boyd	7,316
41		11	(h)	St. Johnstone	W	3-2	Fulton, Nicholas 2	13,236
42		18	(a)	Airdrie	D	0-0		9,000
43		25	(h)	Dunfermline A	W	2-0	McStay, Collins	12,649
44	May	2	(h)	Hibernian	L	1-2	Fulton	25,527

FINAL LEAGUE POSITION : 3rd in Premier Division

Appearances

Sub. Appearances

Goals

Bonner	Morris	Rogan	Grant	Whyte	Wdowczyk	Fulton	Coyne	Cascarino	Nicholas	Collins	Creaney	Galloway	Gillespie	O'Neill	McNally	Miller	Walker	Dziekanowski	McStay	Smith	Mowbray	Marshall	Boyd	#
1	2	3	4	5	6	7†	8	9*	10	11	12	13												1
1	2	3	4	5	6†	7	8*	9	10	11	12	13												2
1	2*	3	4†	5		7	8	9	10	11		12	6	13										3
1	2	3†	4	5	13	7	8		10*	11	9	12	6											4
1	2	3	4	5		7†	8*	9	10	11	12	13	6											5
1				5	3	8			10†	12		9	4	6	11	2	7*		13					6
1			4	13	3	8†			10	12	11	9*	5	6		2	7							7
1	2		4	5	3	8†	9		10	11		6			13	7								8
1	2		4	6	3	8†	9	12	10*	11		5			13	7								9
1			4	5	3		9	12	10*	11†		8	6	13	2	7								10
1			4		3	13	9		10†	11		5	6	8	2	7*		12						11
1	13		3			9	12		10*	11		5	6†	4	2	7			8					12
1	2		3			9	12†		10	11		5*		4	6	7			8	13				13
1	2		4	5	3	13	9		10*		12		11	6	7†			8						14
1			12	6	3		9	13	10*	11		5		4	2	7†			8					15
1	12		6	3			9	13	10*	11		5		4	2	7†			8					16
1	3*		9	13					10*	11	12		4	6	7	2			8		5			17
1				13			9	12	10	11*	4†	3		6	7	2			8		5			18
1			4*	3			9	13	10†		12	5		6	11	2	7		8					19
	13		4	5	3		9		10		12	11		6	2†	7*			8			1		20
			4	5	3		9	7†	10		13	11		6	2				8			1		21
	13			5	3*		9	7	10		12	11	6†	4	2				8			1		22
	6			5	3*		9†	7	10	11			4	2	12				8	13		1		23
	3		4	5			9	7*	10†	11	13			2	6	12			8			1		24
	2		4	6	13		9	12	10†	11				7*	3				8		5	1		25
	2		4†	6	13		9*		10	11	12			7	3				8		5	1		26
	2		4	6	13		9*		10	11	12			7	3				8		5†	1		27
	2			5	3†	13	9		10	11				6	4	7			8			1		28
	2			5	3	13	9*	12	10	11				6	4	7†			8			1		29
	2			5	3		9		10	11				6	4	7			8			1		30
	2			5	13		9	12	10*	11				3	6	4	7†		8			1		31
	2†			5		7	9*	12	10	11				6	4	13			8			1	3	32
	2			5		12	10†		11	9	13			6	4	7*			8			1	3	33
	2			5		7†	9*	12	10	11				6	4				8	13		1	3	34
	2		4*				9		11	10			6	12	7				8		5	1	3	35
				11		12	10	13	9*		2	6	4†			7			8		5	1	3	36
	2			6		12	10*	11	9	13				4	7†				8		5	1	3	37
	8			6	3†	11	12	10	9*	7	4		2			5						1	13	38
	2			6	13	12	10	11	9*	7		4†							8		5	1	3	39
	2			6	13	12	10*	11	9	7		4†							8		5	1	3	40
	2			6	4†		10	11	9	7			13						8		5	1	3	41
	2			6	12		10	11*	9	7	4								8		5	1	3	42
	2		6†	4	12		10	11	9	13					7*				8		5	1	3	43
	2		6	4	12		10	11	9				5	7*					8			1	3	44
19	29	5	20	38	18	18	32	13	32	36	21	26	24	25	21	23			32	1	14	25	12	
3		2	2	1	12	7	11	5	2	11	8		3	3	3	1	1		2	1		1		
1			1		2	15	4	21	11	14	2	2	1	1	2				7		2		1	

57

1992-93

1	Aug	1	(a)	Hearts	W	1-0	Levein (og)	18,510
2		5	(a)	Aberdeen	D	1-1	Creaney	14,618
3		8	(h)	Motherwell	D	1-1	Mowbray	24,935
4		15	(h)	Dundee U	W	2-0	Creaney 2	30,513
5		22	(a)	Rangers	D	1-1	Creaney	43,239
6		29	(a)	Airdrie	D	1-1	Payton	12,222
7	Sep	2	(h)	St. Johnstone	W	3-1	Collins 2, Creaney	21,831
8		12	(h)	Hibernian	L	2-3	Wdowczyk, McStay	28,130
9		19	(a)	Falkirk	W	5-4	Wdowczyk (pen), Creaney 2, Payton, Collins	9,678
10		26	(h)	Partick Thistle	L	1-2	Payton	21,486
11	Oct	3	(a)	Dundee	W	1-0	Galloway	12,866
12		7	(h)	Hearts	D	1-1	Miller	26,049
13		17	(a)	Motherwell	W	3-1	Miller, Galloway (pen), Grant	10,016
14		24	(h)	Airdrie	W	2-0	Collins, McStay	19,549
15		31	(a)	St. Johnstone	D	0-0		9,783
16	Nov	7	(h)	Rangers	L	0-1		51,950
17		11	(a)	Dundee U	D	1-1	Nicholas	11,831
18		21	(h)	Falkirk	W	3-2	Mowbray, Creaney, O'Neil	15,978
19		28	(a)	Hibernian	W	2-1	O'Neil 2	12,985
20	Dec	2	(h)	Aberdeen	D	2-2	Slater, Vata	29,122
21		5	(a)	Partick Thistle	W	3-2	Payton, Grant, Creaney	13,312
22		12	(h)	Dundee	W	1-0	Payton	16,797
23		19	(a)	Hearts	L	0-1		13,554
24		26	(h)	Dundee U	L	0-1		22,852
25	Jan	2	(a)	Rangers	L	0-1		46,039
26		23	(a)	Airdrie	W	1-0	Coyne	7,473
27		30	(h)	Motherwell	D	1-1	McStay	18,513
28	Feb	3	(h)	St. Johnstone	W	5-1	Coyne 2 (2 pens), McAvennie, Wdowczyk, Collins	12,931
29		13	(a)	Aberdeen	D	1-1	Payton	14,673
30		20	(h)	Partick Thistle	D	0-0		15,561
31		23	(a)	Dundee	W	1-0	Payton	7,221
32		27	(a)	Falkirk	W	3-0	McAvennie, Payton 2	8,165
33	Mar	10	(h)	Hearts	W	1-0	Payton	16,984
34		16	(h)	Hibernian	W	2-1	Payton 2	12,178
35		20	(h)	Rangers	W	2-1	Collins, Payton	52,779
36		27	(a)	Dundee U	W	3-2	McAvennie, Galloway, Collins	12,185
37	Apr	3	(a)	Motherwell	L	0-2		10,102
38		6	(h)	Airdrie	W	4-0	Slater, Collins, McAvennie, Vata	10,671
39		10	(a)	St. Johnstone	D	1-1	McAvennie	8,609
40		17	(a)	Hibernian	L	1-3	Nicholas	11,132
41		20	(h)	Falkirk	W	1-0	McAvennie	10,151
42	May	1	(h)	Aberdeen	W	1-0	McAvennie	20,642
43		8	(a)	Partick Thistle	W	1-0	McAvennie (pen)	9,834
44		15	(h)	Dundee	W	2-0	McStay, McAvennie	19,436

FINAL LEAGUE POSITION : 3rd in Premier Division

Appearances

Sub. Appearances

Goals

Marshall G	Morris C	Boyd T	Wdowczyk D	Mowbray A	Gillespie G	O'Neil B	McStay P	Creaney G	Nicholas C	Collins J	Coyne T	Miller J	Whyte D	Galloway M	Payton A	Grant P	McNally M	Slater S	Fulton S	Bonner P	Vata R	McCarrison D	McAvennie F	Smith B	McQuiken J	Gray S	No.
1	2	3	4†	5	6	7	8	9*	10	11	12	14															1
1	2	3	4	5	6†	7	8	9	10*	11	12		14														2
1	2	3	4	5	6	7†	8	9	10*	11	12	14															3
1	2	3†		5	6	14	8		10	11	12	7		4*	9												4
1	2			5		14	8	9		11		7		3	10*	4	6†	12									5
1	2	3		5			8		10	11		7*		6	9	4		12									6
1	2	3†		5		4	8		10*	11				6	9		14	7	12								7
1	2	3		5		4*	8		10	11	12			6	9			7									8
	2	3†		5	6		8		10	11				9		4	14	7		1							9
		3		5	6		8		10*	11		12		14	9	4	2	7		1							10
		3		5			8		10	11				6	12	4	2	9*	14	1	7†						11
		3		5			8		10	11		7*		6	12	4	2	9		1							12
		3		5		14	8		10*	11		7		6†	12	4	2	9		1							13
		3		5			8	12		11		7		6	10*	4	2	9		1			14				14
		3		5	6		8		10	11		7*		2	12	4		9		1							15
	7	3†		5	6	14	8	12	10*	11				2		4		9		1							16
	7	3†		5	6	14	8	12	10	11				2*		4		9		1							17
	2	3		5	6†	4	8	9	10	11					12			7*		1	14						18
		3		5	6	4	8	9*	10†	11					12		2	7		1	14						19
		3		5	6	7	8		10	11					12	4*	2	9		1	14						20
		3		5			8	12	10*	11				9		4	2	7		1	6						21
	2				6		8		10†	3				9		4	5	11*	14	1	7	12					22
		3		5	6*		8	12		11			14	9	10	4	2			1	7†						23
		3		5			8		10*			6	7	4	9	12	2	11†		1	14						24
		3		5*		14	8		10			6	7	4	9†	12	2	11		1							25
		3		5			8	12	10*	11				6			2	7		1		4	9				26
		3		5			8		10	11				6	12		2	7		1		4	9*				27
		3		5			8	12	10	11				6	14		2	7		1		4†	9				28
	2	3	4†				8		10	11				6	12		5	7*		1	14		9				29
	2	3	4				8		10	11				6	12		5	7*		1			9				30
	2	3					8	12		11				6	10		5	7		1		4	9*				31
	2	3					8			11				6	10	4	5	7		1			9				32
	2	3					8			11	12			6	10	4	5	7		1			9*				33
	2	3					8			11				6	10	4	5	7		1			9				34
	2	3					8			11				6	10	4	5	7		1			9				35
	2	3					8		10*	11				6		4	5	7		1	12		9				36
	2	3			6*		8		10	11					12	4	5	7		1			9				37
			6*	3			8		10	11					12	4	5†	7		1	2		9	14			38
		3		5	6		8		10*	11					12	4		7		1	2		9				39
		3†		5*	6		8		10	11					12	4		7		1	2		9	14			40
							8		10*	11				6	12	4		7		1	5		9	2	3		41
1		3									12			6	10*	4		7	8		5		9	2	11		42
1		3	14				8			11		7†		6	10			4			5		9	2			43
1		3		5			8*		10	11		12		6	14			7	4†				9	2			44
11	3	42	24	26	18	11	43	23	12	43	5	10		29	19	27	25	37	3	33	15		19	4	1	1	
		1		6		3	4			5	13	1	1	10	4	2	2	3		7	1		2				
		3	2		3	4	9	2	8	3	2		3	13	2		2				2		9				

59

1993-94

1	Aug	7	(a)	Motherwell	D	2-2	Slater, McAvennie	13,569
2		14	(h)	Hibernian	D	1-1	Nicholas	27,690
3		21	(h)	Rangers	D	0-0		47,942
4		28	(a)	Partick Thistle	W	1-0	McNally	14,013
5	Sep	4	(h)	Aberdeen	L	0-1		34,311
6		11	(a)	Raith R	W	4-1	Nicholas 2, Payton 2	8,114
7		18	(h)	Dundee U	D	1-1	Creaney	26,377
8		25	(a)	Hearts	L	0-1		14,761
9	Oct	2	(h)	Kilmarnock	D	0-0		23,396
10		6	(a)	St. Johnstone	L	1-2	Creaney	7,386
11		9	(h)	Dundee	W	2-1	Creaney, McGinlay	15,980
12		16	(a)	Hibernian	D	1-1	Creaney	14,991
13		30	(a)	Rangers	W	2-1	Collins, O'Neil	47,522
14	Nov	6	(h)	Partick Thistle	W	3-0	McGinlay 2, Nicholas	21,642
15		9	(a)	Aberdeen	D	1-1	O'Neil	19,474
16		13	(a)	Kilmarnock	D	2-2	Nicholas, McGinlay	16,649
17		20	(h)	Hearts	D	0-0		25,990
18		24	(h)	Motherwell	W	2-0	McGinlay 2	16,654
19		27	(h)	Raith R	W	2-0	Collins 2	17,453
20		30	(a)	Dundee U	L	0-1		10,220
21	Dec	4	(h)	St. Johnstone	W	1-0	McGinlay	15,941
22		11	(a)	Dundee	D	1-1	Creaney	8,730
23		18	(h)	Hibernian	W	1-0	McStay	16,808
24	Jan	1	(h)	Rangers	L	2-4	Collins, Nicholas	48,506
25		8	(a)	Partick Thistle	L	0-1		12,887
26		11	(a)	Motherwell	L	1-2	McNally	13,159
27		19	(h)	Aberdeen	D	2-2	Byrne, McStay	19,083
28		22	(h)	Dundee U	D	0-0		17,235
29	Feb	5	(a)	Raith R	D	0-0		7,678
30		12	(a)	Hearts	W	2-0	Nicholas 2	14,049
31	Mar	1	(h)	Kilmarnock	W	1-0	Collins	9,887
32		5	(a)	St. Johnstone	W	1-0	Byrne	8,622
33		19	(a)	Hibernian	D	0-0		14,639
34		26	(h)	Motherwell	L	0-1		36,199
35		30	(h)	Raith R	W	2-1	Donnelly 2	14,140
36	Apr	2	(a)	Dundee U	W	3-1	Falconer, Collins, Mowbray	9,790
37		6	(h)	Dundee	D	1-1	Donnelly	16,585
38		9	(h)	Hearts	D	2-2	Vata, Collins	18,761
39		16	(a)	Kilmarnock	L	0-2		11,499
40		23	(a)	Dundee	W	2-0	McGinlay 2	5,795
41		27	(h)	St. Johnstone	D	1-1	Donnelly	10,602
42		30	(a)	Rangers	D	1-1	Collins	47,018
43	May	7	(h)	Partick Thistle	D	1-1	McGinlay	16,827
44		14	(a)	Aberdeen	D	1-1	Donnelly	16,417

FINAL LEAGUE POSITION : 4th in Premier Division

Appearances

Sub. Appearances

Goals

Bonner P	Boyd T	Wdowczyk D	Grant P	McNally M	Galloway M	Slater S	McStay P	McAvennie F	Creaney G	Collins J	Nicholas C	McGinlay P	Payton A	O'Neil B	Vata R	Mowbray A	Smith B	Gillespie G	Byrne P	Marshall G	McLaughlin B	Biggins W	Martin L	Muggleton	Falconer W	Donnelly S	Hay C	#
1	2	3	4	5	6	7	8	9†	10*	11	12	14																1
1	2	3	4	5	6		8	9*		11	10†	7	12	14														2
1	2	3	4	5	6		8	9*		11	10	7	12															3
1	2	3	4	5	6		8	9*		11	10	7	12															4
1	2	3	4	5	6			9		11†	10*	7	12	14	8													5
1	2	3	4	5		14		9*		11	10	7	12	8†		5												6
1	2	3	4	5	6	11	8		9		10*	7		12														7
1	2	3†	4	5		11	8	9*	10			7		12		5	14											8
1	3*	14	4	5			8		10		12	7	9			11†		2										9
1	3		4	6			8		9		10	7		11*		5		2	12									10
	3		4	5*	6		8		9	11†	10	12		14				2	7	1								11
1	3		4				8		9	11	10	6				5		2	7									12
1	3		4				8		9†	11	10*	6	14	12		5		2	7									13
1	3	2	4				8		9†		10*	6		11	12	5			7		14							14
1	3	5	4				8		9†	11	14	6		10	12			2*	7									15
1	3	2	4*	5	9		8	12			10	6		11		7												16
1	3	5	4				8		9	11	10	6						2	7									17
1	3	5	4				8		7†	11	10	6		9			12	2				14						18
1	3	5	4				8		9*	11	10†	6		7			12	2				14						19
1	3	5	4		14		8		9†	11	10*	6		7				2				12						20
1	3	5	4				8	14	7†	11		6		9				2				10						21
1	3	5	4				8	14	7†	11		6		9				2				10						22
1	3	5	4		14		8			11	12	6		9				2	7†			10*						23
1	3	5†	4	12			8			11	10	6		9*				2	7			14						24
1	3		4*	5	6		8		9†	11	10			14			12	2	7									25
1	3		4	6	12		8		14	10	9			11		5		2*	7†									26
1			6	14			8			11	10	4		12		5		2†	7			9*	3					27
	3			6			8			11	10	9		12		5		2	7*			4	1					28
	3			6			8	9†		11	4	10				5		12	7*			14	2	1				29
	3			4			8			11	9	6	12	14	5		2	7*				1		10†				30
	3			6						11	9	7	8		5		2*	12				4	1	10				31
	3		2	14			8			11	9	6†			5		12	7*				4	1	10				32
	3		4				8			11	9†	6			5			7				2	1	10	14			33
	3		4				8			11	9	6	14		5		2†	7*				1	10	12				34
	3			4†			8			11		6	14		5			7*	12			2	1	10	9			35
	3		8	4†						11		6*	14	7	5				12			2	1	10	9			36
	3		4	10			8			11		6*		7		5			12			2	1		9			37
	3		4	14			8			11	6†			7		5						2	1	10	9			38
	3		4	2*			8			11	12	6		7		5			14				1	10	9			39
1		5	4	2						11	8	6				3						7		10	9			40
1		5	4	2*						11	8†	6	14			3			12			7		10	9			41
1		7	4	6						11		8†			5	2		12	14			3		10	9*			42
1		6	12	4						11		8			5*	2			14			3†		10	9	7		43
1		4	12							11		8			5	2	6*	14				3		10	9	7†		44
31	38	24	27	30	16	3	35	8	17	38	30	39	1	14	6	20	6	25	18	1	4	15	12	14	10	2		
	1	1	2	6	1		3	1		5	2	6	14	4	2	1	2	4		8	5				2			
		2		1	2	1	5	8	8	10	2	2	1	1		2						1	5					

61

1994-95

1	Aug	13	(a)	Falkirk	D	1-1	Walker	12,635
2		20	(h)	Dundee U	W	2-1	Walker, Mowbray	25,817
3		27	(a)	Rangers	W	2-0	Collins, McStay	44,607
4	Sep	10	(a)	Partick Th	W	2-1	O'Donnell 2	14,439
5		17	(h)	Kilmarnock	D	1-1	McGinlay	28,457
6		24	(h)	Hibernian	W	2-0	O'Donnell, Collins	28,170
7	Oct	1	(a)	Motherwell	D	1-1	Walker	10,869
8		8	(h)	Aberdeen	D	0-0		29,454
9		15	(a)	Hearts	L	0-1		12,086
10		22	(h)	Falkirk	L	0-2		23,688
11		30	(h)	Rangers	L	1-3	Byrne	32,171
12	Nov	5	(a)	Dundee U	D	2-2	Collins 2	10,496
13		9	(h)	Partick Th	D	0-0		21,462
14		19	(a)	Kilmarnock	D	0-0		13,932
15		30	(a)	Hibernian	D	1-1	Collins	12,295
16	Dec	3	(h)	Motherwell	D	2-2	Falconer, Philliben (og)	21,465
17		26	(a)	Aberdeen	D	0-0		19,206
18		31	(h)	Falkirk	W	2-0	Grant, Walker	21,294
19	Jan	4	(a)	Rangers	D	1-1	Byrne	45,794
20		7	(h)	Dundee U	D	1-1	Collins	21,436
21		11	(h)	Hearts	D	1-1	Van Hooijdonk	26,491
22		14	(h)	Kilmarnock	W	2-1	Falconer, Collins	25,342
23		21	(a)	Partick Th	D	0-0		11,904
24	Feb	4	(a)	Motherwell	L	0-1		10,771
25		11	(h)	Hibernian	D	2-2	Collins, Falconer	24,284
26		25	(a)	Hearts	D	1-1	O'Donnell	11,185
27	Mar	5	(h)	Aberdeen	W	2-0	Van Hooijdonk 2	20,621
28		21	(a)	Kilmarnock	W	1-0	Walker	10,112
29	Apr	1	(h)	Motherwell	D	1-1	Walker	24,047
30		15	(a)	Aberdeen	L	0-2		16,668
31		19	(h)	Hearts	L	0-1		18,638
32		29	(a)	Falkirk	W	2-1	O'Donnell, Boyd	9,714
33	May	2	(h)	Partick Th	L	1-3	Grant	18,963
34		7	(h)	Rangers	W	3-0	Van Hooijdonk, Moore (og), Vata	31,025
35		9	(a)	Hibernian	D	1-1	Falconer	6,019
36		13	(a)	Dundee U	W	1-0	O'Donnell	10,993

FINAL LEAGUE POSITION : 4th in Premier Division

Appearances

Sub. Appearances

Goals

Marshall	Martin	Boyd	McNally	Mowbray	Grant	Galloway	McStay	Falconer	Walker	Collins	Nicholas	Donnelly	McGinlay	O'Neil	O'Donnell	McLaughlin	Smith	Byrne	McKinlay	O'Neill	Gray	Bonner	Hay	Slavin	Van Hooijdonk	Vata	Mackay	
1	2	3	4	5	6	7	8	9	10	11																		1
1	2	3	4	5	6		8	9*	10	11	7†	12	14															2
1		3	4	5	2	7	8		10	11	12	9*	6†	14														3
1		3	4	5	2	7†			10	11*	12	9	6		8	14												4
1	2†	3	4	5	6		8		9	11		14	7		10													5
1		3	4	5	6	2			10*	11	9†	12	7	14	8													6
1		3	4		6	2	12	14	10	11*	9†		7	5	8													7
1		3	4			2	8	14	10*	11	12	9		7	5†	6												8
1		3	4		6	2*	8*	14	10	11	12	9†		7			5											9
1	2*	3†	4		6			9	12	11	10	14	7	5	8													10
1		3	4				8	14	10	11	12	9		5	6				2†	7*								11
1		2		4	6		8	9	10	11	12	14			5				7*	3†								12
1		2	12	5	6		8			11	10	9†		4					7	3*	14							13
1		2	4		6		8	9	10*	11		12		5	7					3								14
1		2	4		6		8	9	10	11*				5		7				3	12							15
1		2			6	4	8	9	10		12			5		7*				3	11							16
		2		5	6		8			10	11		14	4		9				3		1	7†					17
		2			6		8			10	11			4		9	5			3†	14	1	7					18
		2					5	8	10	11				4	6	9		7*			3	1	12					19
		2					8	12	10*	11				4	6	9		7†			3	1	14	5				20
		2					4	8	12	11					6	10		7*			3	1		5	9			21
		2	4				8	10		11					6	7†					3	1	14	5	9			22
		2	5		6			10		11				4	8	7					3	1			9			23
		2	5		6		8	10		11				4	7	14					3†	1			9			24
		2	5		6			10		11				4	8	7					3	1			9			25
		2	5	6				10	12	11				4	8	7				3		1			9*			26
		2		5	6			8	10		12			4	11	7*				3		1			9			27
		2		5	12		8	10†	14	11				6	7*					3		1			9	4		28
		2		5			8	12	10	11				6*	7					3		1			9	4		29
		2			6		8	9	10*	11		12		5	14	7				3†		1				4		30
		3		5	6		9	10*	11		12			4	8	7					1					2		31
		2		5	6		8	9	10†	11				4	7					3		1		14				32
		2		5	6		8	9		11				4	7					3		1		10				33
		2			6		8	12		11		10*		5	14	7				3		1		9†		4		34
		2			6		8	10						5	11	7				3		1		9		4		35
		2			6†		8			11	12			10	7*					3	14	1		9	4	5		36
16	4	35	19	15	27	11	28	19	22	33	5	7	7	24	25	19	3	6	17	8	20	2	3	13	7	1		
		1		1		1	7	4	1	7	10	1	2	2	2				1		3		3		1			
		1		1	2		1	4	6	8				1		6			2					4	1			

63

SCOTTISH F.A. CUP

1970/71 SEASON
3rd Round
Jan 23 vs Queen of the South (h) 5-1
Att: 25,900 Hood 2, Wallace, Callaghan, McNeill
4th Round
Feb 13 vs Dunfermline Athletic (h) 1-1
Att: 37,000 Wallace
Replay
Feb 17 vs Dunfermline Athletic (a) 1-0
Att: 22,728 Hood
5th Round
Mar 6 vs Raith Rovers (h) 7-1
Att: 32,000 Lennox 3, Davidson, Wallace, Gemmell (pen), Callaghan
Semi-Final (at Hampden Park)
Apr 3 vs Airdrieonians 3-3
Att: 39,404 Hood 2, Johnstone
Replay (at Hampden Park)
Apr 7 vs Aidrieonians 2-0
Att: 47,180 Hood, Johnstone
FINAL (at Hampden Park)
May 8 vs Rangers 1-1
Att: 120,092 Lennox
Replay (at Hampden Park)
May 12 vs Rangers 2-1
Att: 103,332 Macari, Hood (pen)

1971/72 SEASON
3rd Round
Feb 5 vs Albion Rovers (h) 5-0
Att: 20,212 Macari, Deans, Callaghan 2, Murdoch
4th Round
Feb 26 vs Dundee (h) 4-0
Att: 47,500 Lennox 2, Dalglish, Deans
5th Round
Mar 18 vs Heart of Midlothian (h) 1-1
Att: 47,500 Deans
Replay
Mar 27 vs Heart of Midlothian (a) 1-0
Att: 40,029 Macari
Semi-Final (at Hampden Park)
Apr 12 vs Kilmarnock 3-1
Att: 48,398 Deans 2, Macari
FINAL (at Hampden Park)
May 6 vs Hibernian 6-1
Att: 106,102 McNeill, Deans 3, Macari 2

1972/73 SEASON
3rd Round
Feb 3 vs East Fife (h) 4-1
Att: 25,000 Deans 2, Dalglish 2
4th Round
Feb 24 vs Motherwell (a) 4-0
Att: 24,764 Deans 2, Dalglish, Lennox
5th Round
Mar 17 vs Aberdeen (h) 0-0
Att: 40,000
Replay
Mar 21 vs Aberdeen (a) 1-0
Att: 33,465 McNeill
Semi-Final (at Hampden Park)
Apr 7 vs Dundee 0-0
Att: 53,428
Replay (at Hampden Park)
Apr 11 vs Dundee 3-0 (aet.)
Att: 47,384 Johnstone 2, Dalglish
FINAL (at Hampden Park)
May 5 vs Rangers 2-3
Att: 122,714 Dalglish, Connelly (pen)

1973/74 SEASON
3rd Round
Jan 27 vs Clydebank (h) 6-1
Att: 28,000 Deans 3, Lennox 2, Davidson

4th Round
Feb 17 vs Stirling Albion (h) 6-1
Att: 23,000 Hood 2, Murray 2, Dalglish, Wilson
5th Round
Mar 10 vs Motherwell (h) 2-2
Att: 46,000 Hood 2
Replay
Mar 13 vs Motherwell (a) 1-0
Att: 24,875 Deans
Semi-Final (at Hampden Park)
Apr 3 vs Dundee 1-0
Att: 58,250 Johnstone
FINAL (at Hampden Park)
May 4 vs Dundee United 3-0
Att: 75,959 Hood, Murray, Deans

1974/75 SEASON
3rd Round
Jan 25 vs Hibernian (a) 2-0
Att: 36,210 Deans, Murray
4th Round
Feb 15 vs Clydebank (h) 4-1
Att: 21,000 Dalglish 2, McNamara, McDonald
5th Round
Mar 8 vs Dumbarton (a) 2-1
Att: 16,000 Glavin, Wilson
Semi-Final (at Hampden Park)
Apr 2 vs Dundee 1-0
Att: 40,702 Glavin
FINAL (at Hampden Park)
May 3 vs Airdrieonians 3-1
Att: 3-1 Wilson 2, P. McCluskey (pen)

1975/76 SEASON
3rd Round
Jan 24 vs Motherwell (a) 2-3
Att: 25,000 Dalglish, Lynch

1976/77 SEASON
3rd Round
Jan 29 vs Airdrieonians (a) 1-1
Att: 18,316 Doyle
Replay
Feb 2 vs Airdrieonians (h) 5-0
Att: 20,000 Craig 4, Glavin
4th Round
Feb 27 vs Ayr United (h) 1-1
Att: 38,000 Glavin
Replay
Mar 2 vs Ayr United (a) 3-1
Att: 13,100 Glavin (pen), Doyle, Aitken
5th Round
Mar 13 vs Queen of the South (h) 5-1
Att: 27,000 Glavin 3 (2 pens), Craig, Dalglish
Semi-Final (at Hampden Park)
Apr 6 vs Dundee 2-0
Att: 29,900 Craig 2
FINAL (at Hampden Park)
May 7 vs Rangers 1-0
Att: 54,252 Lynch (pen)

1977/78 SEASON
3rd Round
Feb 6 vs Dundee (h) 7-1
Att: 22,000 McCluskey 3, Burns, MacDonald, McAdam 2
4th Round
Feb 27 vs Kilmarnock (h) 1-1
Att: 25,000 MacDonald
Replay
Mar 6 vs Kilmarnock (a) 0-1
Att: 14,100

1978/79 SEASON
3rd Round
Jan 31 vs Montrose (a) 4-2
Att: 3,066 McCluskey 3, Lynch (pen)
4th Round
Feb 26 vs Berwick Rangers (h) 3-0
Att: 13,000 Lynch (pen), Burns, McDowell (og)
Quarter-Final
Mar 10 vs Aberdeen (a) 1-1
Att: 24,000 Doyle
Replay
Mar 14 vs Aberdeen (h) 1-2
Att: 37,000 Lennox

1979/80 SEASON
3rd Round
Jan 26 vs Raith Rovers (h) 2-1
Att: 18,000 Lennox, Doyle
4th Round
Feb 16 vs St. Mirren (h) 1-1
Att: 32,000 MacLeod
Replay
Feb 20 vs St. Mirren (a) 3-2 (aet.) (90 minutes 2-2)
Att: 27,166 Doyle 2, Lennox (pen)
Quarter-Final
Mar 8 vs Morton (h) 2-0
Att: 35,000 Casey, McCluskey
Semi-Final (at Hampden Park)
Apr 12 vs Hibernian 5-0
Att: 32,925 Lennox, Provan, Doyle, McAdam, MacLeod
FINAL (at Hampden Park)
May 10 vs Rangers 1-0 (aet.)
Att: 70,303 McCluskey

1980/81 SEASON
3rd Round
Jan 24 vs Berwick Rangers (a) 2-0
Att: 9,676 Nicholas, Burns
4th Round
Feb 14 vs Stirling Albion (h) 3-0
Att: 14,200 McGarvey, McCluskey, Burns
Quarter-Final
Mar 8 vs East Stirlingshire (h) 2-0
Att: 18,500 Conroy, MacLeod
Semi-Final (at Hampden Park)
Apr 11 vs Dundee United 0-0
Att: 40,337
Replay (at Hampden Park)
Apr 15 vs Dundee United 2-3
Att: 32,328 Nicholas 2 (1 pen)

1981/82 SEASON
3rd Round
Jan 23 vs Queen of the South (h) 4-0
Att: 11,282 McGarvey, McGrain, McCluskey (pen), Halpin
4th Round
Feb 13 vs Aberdeen (a) 0-1
Att: 24,000

1982/83 SEASON
3rd Round
Jan 28 vs Clydebank (a) 3-0
Att: 9,950 Nicholas 2, McCluskey
4th Round
Feb 19 vs Dunfermline Athletic (h) 3-0
Att: 12,374 McGarvey 2, McCluskey
Quarter-Final
Mar 12 vs Heart of Midlothian (h) 4-1
Att: 25,458 Nicholas 2, MacLeod, McGarvey
Semi-Final (at Hampden Park)
Apr 16 vs Aberdeen 0-1
Att: 51,152

1983/84 SEASON
3rd Round
Jan 28 vs Berwick Rangers (a) 4-0
Att: 5,510 McClair 2, McGarvey, Melrose
4th Round
Feb 18 vs East Fife (a) 6-0
Att: 10,000 Burns 2, McGarvey, Colquhoun, McClair, MacLeod
Quarter-Final
Mar 17 vs Motherwell (a) 6-0
Att: 14,795 McClair 2, Reid, Burns, McGarvey, MacLeod
Semi-Final (at Hampden Park)
Apr 14 vs St. Mirren 2-1
Att: 24,690 McClair, P. McStay
FINAL (at Hampden Park)
May 19 vs Aberdeen 1-2 (aet.)
Att: 58,900 P. McStay

1984/85 SEASON
3rd Round
Jan 30 vs Hamilton Academical (a) 2-1
Att: 10,000 McGarvey 2
4th Round
Feb 16 vs Inverness Thistle (h) 6-0
Att: 14,927 P. McStay, Johnston, McGarvey, MacLeod
Quarter-Final
Mar 9 vs Dundee (a) 1-1
Att: 21,301 Johnston
Replay
Mar 13 vs Dundee (h) 2-1
Att: 37,390 McGarvey, Johnston
Semi-Final (at Hampden Park)
Apr 13 vs Motherwell 1-1
Att: 30,536 Burns
Replay (at Hampden Park)
Apr 17 vs Motherwell 3-0
Att: 25,677 Johnston 2, Aitken
FINAL (at Hampden Park)
May 18 vs Dundee United 2-1
Att: 60,346 Provan, McGarvey

1985/86 SEASON
3rd Round
Jan 25 vs St. Johnstone (h) 2-0
Att: 15,006 Grant, Johnston
4th Round
Feb 15 vs Queen's Park (h) 2-1
Att: 11,656 McClair, Aitken
Quarter-Final
Mar 8 vs Hibernian (a) 3-4
Att: 20,000 McClair 2 (1 pen), McGhee

1986/87 SEASON
3rd Round
Feb 1 vs Aberdeen (a) 2-2
Att: 23,000 McClair, McInally
Replay
Feb 4 vs Aberdeen (h) 0-0 (aet.)
Att: 55,405
2nd Replay (at Dens Park, Dundee)
Feb 9 vs Aberdeen 1-0
Att: 21,255 McClair
4th Round
Feb 21 vs Heart of Midlothian (a) 0-1
Att: 28,891

1987/88 SEASON
3rd Round
Jan 30 vs Stranraer (h) 1-0
Att: 21,625 McAvennie
4th Round
Feb 21 vs Hibernian (h) 0-0
Att: 30,577
Replay
Feb 24 vs Hibernian (a) 1-0
Att: 24,000 Stark

Quarter-Final
Mar 12 vs Partick Thistle (a) 3-0
Att: 16,800 Walker, Burns, Stark
Semi-Final (at Hampden Park)
Apr 9 vs Heart of Midlothian 2-1
Att: 65,886 McGhee, Walker
FINAL (at Hampden Park)
May 14 vs Dundee United 2-1
Att: 74,000 McAvennie 2

1988/89 SEASON
3rd Round
Jan 28 vs Dumbarton (h) 2-0
Att: 24,844 Walker, Burns
4th Round
Feb 18 vs Clydebank (h) 4-1
Att: 23,141 Burns 2, McAvennie, Stark
Quarter-Final
Mar 18 vs Heart of Midlothian (h) 2-1
Att: 46,348 McGhee, Aitken (pen)
Semi-Final (at Hampden Park)
Apr 16 vs Hibernian 3-1
Att: 42,160 McCarthy, McGhee, Walker
FINAL (at Hampden Park)
May 20 vs Rangers 1-0
Att: 72,069 Miller

1989/90 SEASON
3rd Round
Jan 20 vs Forfar Athletic (a) 2-1
Att: 8,388 Morris (pen), Dziekanowski
4th Round
Feb 24 vs Rangers (h) 1-0
Att: 52,565 Coyne
Quarter-Final
Mar 17 vs Dunfermline Athletic (a) 0-0
Att: 19,568
Replay
Mar 24 vs Dunfermline Athletic (h) 3-0
Att: 40,798 McStay, Coyne, Miller
Semi-Final (at Hampden Park)
Apr 14 vs Clydebank 2-0
Att: 34,768 Walker 2
FINAL (at Hampden Park)
May 12 vs Aberdeen 0-0 (aet).
Att: 60,493 Aberdeen won 9-8 on penalties

1990/91 SEASON
3rd Round
Jan 26 vs Forfar Athletic (a) 2-0
Att: 8,000 Wdowczyk, Coyne
4th Round
Feb 26 vs St. Mirren (h) 3-0
Att: 27,189 Miller, Creaney, McWhirter (og)
Quarter-Final
Mar 17 vs Rangers (h) 2-0
Att: 52,286 Creaney, Wdowczyk
Semi-Final (at Hampden Park)
Apr 3 vs Motherwell 0-0
Att: 41,765
Replay (at Hampden Park)
Apr 9 vs Motherwell 2-4
Att: 31,371 Boyd (og), Rogan

1991/92 SEASON
3rd Round
Jan 22 vs Montrose (h) 6-0
Att: 18,578 Creaney 3, Coyne 3
4th Round
Feb 11 vs Dundee United (h) 2-2
Att: 26,225 Creaney, Coyne
Quarter-Final
Mar 3 vs Greenock Morton (h) 3-0
Att: 28,016 Creaney 2, Collins
Semi-Final (at Hampden Park)
Mar 31 vs Rangers 0-1
Att: 45,191

1992/93 SEASON
3rd Round
Jan 9 vs Clyde (a) 0-0
Att: 7,000
Replay
Jan 20 vs Clyde (h) 1-0
Att: 16,559 Coyne
4th Round
Feb 6 vs Falkirk (a) 0-2
Att: 13,012

1993/94 SEASON
3rd Round
Jan 29 vs Motherwell (a) 0-1
Att: 14,061

1994/95 SEASON
3rd Round
Jan 28 vs St. Mirren (h) 2-0
Att: 28,449 Falconer, Van Hooijdonk
4th Round
Feb 18 vs Meadowbank Thistle (h) 3-0
Att: 23,710 Van Hooijdonk 2, Falconer
Quarter-Final
Mar 10 vs Kilmarnock (h) 1-0
Att: 30,881 Collins
Semi-Final (at Ibrox Stadium)
Apr 7 vs Hibernian 0-0
Att: 40,950
Replay (at Ibrox Stadium)
Apr 11 vs Hibernian 3-1
Att: 32,410 Falconer, Collins, O'Donnell
FINAL (at Hampden Park)
May 27 vs Airdrieonians 1-0
Att: 36,915 Van Hooijdonk

SCOTTISH LEAGUE CUP
1970/71 SEASON
Preliminary Round, Game One
Aug 8 vs Heart of Midlothian (a) 2-1
Att: 32,000 Hughes, Johnstone
Preliminary Round, Game Two
Aug 12 vs Clyde (h) 5-3
Att: 25,000 Lennox 3, Johnstone 2
Preliminary Round, Game Three
Aug 15 vs Dundee United (h) 2-2
Att: 39,000 Callaghan, Lennox
Preliminary Round, Game Four
Aug 19 vs Clyde (a) 2-0
Att: 24,000 Gemmell 2 (2 pens)
Preliminary Round, Game Five
Aug 22 vs Heart of Midlothian (h) 4-2
Att: 40,000 Hughes 2, Connelly, Macari
Preliminary Round, Game Six
Aug 26 vs Dundee United (a) 2-2
Att: 16,000 Hay, Macari
Quarter-Final (1st leg)
Sep 9 vs Dundee (a) 2-2
Att: 23,000 Johnstone 2
Quarter-Final (2nd leg)
Sep 23 vs Dundee (h) 5-1 (aggregate 7-3)
Att: 41,000 Macari 2, Hughes, Hood, Wilson
Semi-Final (at Hampden Park)
Oct 7 vs Dumbarton 0-0 (aet.)
Att: 25,838
Replay (at Hampden Park)
Oct 12 vs Dumbarton 4-3 (aet) (90 mins 2-2)
Att: 32,913 Lennox 2, Wallace, Macari
FINAL (at Hampden Park)
Oct 24 vs Rangers 0-1
Att: 106,263

1971/72 SEASON

Preliminary Round, Game One
Aug 14 vs Rangers (h) 2-0
Att: 72,500 (at Ibrox) Johnstone, Dalglish (pen)

Preliminary Round, Game Two
Aug 18 vs Morton (a) 1-0
Att: 20,000 Lennox

Preliminary Round, Game Three
Aug 21 vs Ayr United (a) 3-0
Att: 20,000 Hughes, Hay, Dalglish

Preliminary Round, Game Four
Aug 25 vs Morton (h) 0-1
Att: 27,000

Preliminary Round, Game Five
Aug 28 vs Rangers (a) 3-0
Att: 74,000 Dalglish, Callaghan, Lennox

Preliminary Round, Game Six
Aug 30 vs Ayr United (h) 4-1
Att: 16,500 Dalglish, Lennox, Hay, Macari

Quarter-Final (1st leg)
Sep 8 vs Clydebank (a) 5-0
Att: 10,000 Macari 2, Hood, Callaghan, White

Quarter-Final (2nd leg)
Sep 22 vs Clydebank (h) 6-2 (agg. 11-2)
Att: 16,000 Hood 3, Macari 2, Ruddy (og)

Semi-Final (at Hampden Park)
Oct 6 vs St. Mirren 3-0
Att: 29,488 Hay, Hood, Lennox

FINAL (at Hampden Park)
Oct 23 vs Partick Thistle 1-4
Att: 62,740 Dalglish

1972/73 SEASON

Preliminary Round, Game One
Aug 12 vs Stirling Albion (a) 3-0
Att: 1,000 Macari 2, Dalglish

Preliminary Round, Game Two
Aug 16 vs East Fife (h) 1-1
Att: 15,000 Dalglish

Preliminary Round, Game Three
Aug 19 vs Arbroath (a) 5-0
Att: 7,607 Dalglish 2, Deans 2, Murdoch (pen)

Preliminary Round, Game Four
Aug 23 vs East Fife (a) 3-2
Att: 9,521 Dalglish 2, Lennox

Preliminary Round, Game Five
Aug 26 vs Stirling Albion (h) 3-0
Att: 17,000 Dalglish, Deans, Murdoch (pen)

Preliminary Round, Game Six
Aug 28 vs Arbroath (h) 3-3
Att: 4,962 Dalglish, Hood, Cargill (og)

2nd Round (1st leg)
Sep 20 vs Stranraer (a) 2-1
Att: 4,500 Lennox, Davidson

2nd Round (2nd leg)
Oct 4 vs Stranraer (h) 5-2 (aggregate 7-3)
Att: 9,000 Lennox 2, Deans, Davidson, Murdoch (pen)

Quarter-Final (1st leg)
Oct 11 vs Dundee (a) 0-1
Att: 21,938

Quarter-Final (2nd leg)
Nov 1 vs Dundee (h) 3-2 (aet.) (agg. 3-3)
Att: 39,000 Macari 2, Lennox

Replay (at Hampden Park)
Nov 20 vs Dundee 4-1
Att: 36,483 Deans 2, Dalglish, Hood

Semi-Final (at Hampden Park)
Nov 27 vs Aberdeen 3-2
Att: 39,680 Johnstone, Callaghan, Hood (pn)

FINAL (at Hampden Park)
Dec 9 vs Hibernian 1-2
Att: 71,696 Dalglish

1973/74 SEASON

Preliminary Round, Game One
Aug 11 vs Arbroath (h) 2-1
Att: 19,000 Lennox, Lynch

Preliminary Round, Game Two
Aug 15 vs Falkirk (a) 2-0
Att: 12,000 Lennox (pen), Lynch

Preliminary Round, Game Three
Aug 18 vs Rangers (a) 2-1
Att: 63,173 Lennox, Hood

Preliminary Round, Game Four
Aug 22 vs Falkirk (h) 2-1
Att: 14,000 Lennox 2 (1 pen)

Preliminary Round, Game Five
Aug 25 vs Rangers (h) 1-3
Att: 57,000 Lennox

Preliminary Round, Game Six
Aug 29 vs Arbroath (a) 3-1
Att: 5,101 Lennox, Dalglish, Wilson

2nd Round (1st leg)
Sep 12 vs Motherwell (a) 2-1
Att: 19,253 Hood, Murray

2nd Round (2nd leg)
Oct 10 vs Motherwell (h) 0-1 (aet) (agg 2-2)
Att: 24,000

Replay
Oct 29 vs Motherwell (h) 3-2
Att: 26,000 Murray, Deans, Johnstone

Quarter-Final (1st leg)
Oct 31 vs Aberdeen (h) 3-2
Att: 28,000 Dalglish 2, McCluskey

Quarter-Final (2nd leg)
Nov 21 vs Aberdeen (a) 0-0 (aggregate 3-2)
Att: 16,000

Semi-Final (at Hampden Park)
Dec 5 vs Rangers 3-1
Att: 54,864 Hood 3

FINAL (at Hampden Park)
Dec 15 vs Dundee 0-1
Att: 27,974

1974/75 SEASON

Preliminary Round, Game One
Aug 10 vs Motherwell (h) 2-1
Att: 27,000 Dalglish, Wilson

Preliminary Round, Game Two
Aug 14 vs Ayr United (a) 2-3
Att: 6,500 Murray, Connelly

Preliminary Round, Game Three
Aug 17 vs Dundee United (h) 1-0
Att: 26,000 McNamara

Preliminary Round, Game Four
Aug 21 vs Ayr United (h) 5-2
Att: 16,000 Johnstone, Wilson 2, Lennox

Preliminary Round, Game Five
Aug 24 vs Dundee United (a) 1-0
Att: 15,500 Wilson

Preliminary Round, Game Six
Aug 28 vs Motherwell (a) 2-2
Att: 8,747 Dalglish 2

Quarter-Final (1st leg)
Sep 11 vs Hamilton Academical (h) 2-0
Att: 12,000 Hood 2

Quarter-Final (2nd leg)
Sep 25 vs Hamilton Acad. (a) 4-2 (agg. 6-2)
Att: 8,000 Deans, Callaghan (pen), McNamara, Lennox

Semi-Final (at Hampden Park)
Oct 9 vs Airdrieonians 1-0
Att: 19,332 Murray

FINAL (at Hampden Park)
Oct 26 vs Hibernian 6-3
Att: 53,848 Deans 3, Wilson, Murray, Johnstone

1975/76 SEASON

Preliminary Round, Game One
Aug 9 vs Aberdeen (h) 1-0
Att: 32,000 Dalglish

Preliminary Round, Game Two
Aug 13 vs Heart of Midlothian (a) 0-2
Att: 19,000

Preliminary Round, Game Three
Aug 16 vs Dumbarton (h) 3-1
Att: 23,000 Wilson, Lennox, Edvaldsson

Preliminary Round, Game Four
Aug 20 vs Heart of Midlothian (h) 3-1
Att: 28,000 Glavin, Lynch, Edvaldsson

Preliminary Round, Game Five
Aug 23 vs Dumbarton (a) 8-0
Att: 12,500 Hood 2, Wilson 2, Dalglish 2, Callaghan, McGrain

Preliminary Round, Game Six
Aug 27 vs Aberdeen (a) 2-0
Att: 13,000 Lennox, Ritchie

Quarter-Final (1st leg)
Sep 10 vs Stenhousemuir (a) 2-0
Att: 4,701 Lennox, Dalglish

Quarter-Final (2nd leg)
Sep 24 vs Stenhousemuir (h) 1-0 (agg. 3-0)
Att: 6,000 Lynch

Semi-Final (at Hampden Park)
Oct 6 vs Partick Thistle 1-0
Att: 31,421 Edvaldsson

FINAL (at Hampden Park)
Oct 25 vs Rangers 0-1
Att: 58,806

1976/77 SEASON

Preliminary Round, Game One
Aug 14 vs Dundee United (a) 1-0
Att: 13,000 Dalglish

Preliminary Round, Game Two
Aug 18 vs Dumbarton (h) 3-0
Att: 15,000 Dalglish 2 (2 pens), Doyle

Preliminary Round, Game Three
Aug 21 vs Arbroath (a) 5-0
Att: 6,826 Dalglish, Wilson, McGrain, Glavin, Edvaldsson

Preliminary Round, Game Four
Aug 25 vs Dumbarton (a) 3-3
Att: 12,000 Wilson, MacDonald, Doyle

Preliminary Round, Game Five
Aug 28 vs Arbroath (h) 2-1
Att: 17,000 Wilson, Doyle

Preliminary Round, Game Six
Sep 1 vs Dundee United (h) 1-1
Att: 15,000 MacDonald

Quarter-Final (1st leg)
Sep 22 vs Albion Rovers (a) 1-0
Att: 8,000 Callaghan

Quarter-Final (2nd leg)
Oct 6 vs Albion Rovers (h) 5-0 (agg. 6-0)
Att: 7,000 Dalglish 3 (1pen), Doyle 2

Semi-Final (at Hampden Park)
Oct 26 vs Heart of Midlothian 2-1
Att: 21,706 Dalglish 2 (1 pen)

FINAL (at Hampden Park)
Nov 6 vs Aberdeen 1-2
Att: 69,707 Dalglish (pen)

1977/78 SEASON

2nd Round (1st leg)
Aug 31 vs Motherwell (h) 0-0
Att: 23,000

2nd Round (2nd leg)
Sep 3 vs Motherwell (a) 4-2 (aggregate 4-2)
Att: 20,494 Wilson, Burns, Craig, McLaren (og)

3rd Round (1st leg)
Oct 5 vs Stirling Albion (a) 2-1
Att: 8,600 Doyle, Aitken
3rd Round (2nd leg)
Oct 26 vs Stirling Albion (h) 1-1 (agg. 3-2)
Att: 12,000 Kennedy (og)
Quarter-Final (1st leg)
Nov 9 vs St. Mirren (a) 3-1
Att: 18,101 Craig 2, Edvaldsson
Quarter-Final (2nd leg)
Nov 16 vs St. Mirren (h) 2-0 (aggregate 5-1)
Att: 17,000 Wilson, Doyle
Semi-Final (at Hampden Park)
Mar 1 vs Heart of Midlothian 2-0
Att: 18,840 Craig, McCluskey
FINAL (at Hampden Park)
Mar 18 vs Rangers 1-2 (aet.)
Att: 60,168 Edvaldsson

1978/79 SEASON
1st Round (1st leg)
Aug 16 vs Dundee (h) 3-1
Att: 12,000 McAdam 2, Glavin
1st Round (2nd leg)
Aug 23 vs Dundee (a) 3-0 (aggregate 6-1)
Att: 12,698 Doyle 2, Conn
2nd Round (1st leg)
Aug 30 vs Dundee United (a) 3-2
Att: 12,648 Lynch, MacDonald, Conroy
2nd Round (2nd leg)
Sep 2 vs Dundee United (h) 1-0 (agg. 4-2)
Att: 30,000 Glavin (pen)
3rd Round (1st leg)
Oct 4 vs Motherwell (h) 0-1
Att: 19,000
3rd Round (2nd leg)
Oct 11 vs Motherwell (a) 4-1 (agg. 4-2)
Att: 17,911 McAdam 2, Lennox, Aitken
Quarter-Final (1st leg)
Nov 8 vs Montrose (a) 1-1
Att: 3,872 Lynch (pen)
Quarter-Final (2nd leg)
Nov 15 vs Montrose (h) 3-1 (aggregate 4-2)
Att: 10,000 Lynch (pen), McAdam, Edvaldsson
Semi-Final (at Hampden Park)
Dec 13 vs Rangers 2-3 (aet.) (90 mins. 2-2)
Att: 49,432 Doyle, McAdam

1979/80 SEASON
2nd Round (1st leg)
Aug 29 vs Falkirk (a) 2-1
Att: 9,000 Lennox, Doyle
2nd Round (2nd leg)
Sep 1 vs Falkirk (h) 4-1 (aggregate 6-2)
Att: 17,000 Conroy 2, Lennox, Doyle
3rd Round (1st leg)
Sep 26 vs Stirling Albion (a) 2-1
Att: 8,000 McAdam, Doyle
3rd Round (2nd leg)
Oct 10 vs Stirling Albion (h) 2-0 (agg. 4-1)
Att: 11,000 MacLeod (pen), Doyle
Quarter-Final (1st leg)
Oct 31 vs Aberdeen (a) 2-3
Att: 24,000 Edvaldsson, Provan
Quarter-Final (2nd leg)
Nov 24 vs Aberdeen (h) 0-1 (aggregate 2-4)
Att: 39,000

1980/81 SEASON
2nd Round (1st leg)
Aug 27 vs Stirling Albion (a) 0-1
Att: 5,800
2nd Round (2nd leg)
Aug 30 vs Stirling Alb. (h) 6-1 (aet) (agg 6-2)
Att: 16,000 Burns 2, Nicholas 2, Provan, Sullivan

3rd Round (1st leg)
Sep 22 vs Hamilton Academical (a) 3-1
Att: 9,500 Burns, Nicholas, Doyle
3rd Round (2nd leg)
Sep 24 vs Hamilton Acad. (h) 4-1 (agg. 7-2)
Att: 10,000 McGarvey 2, Burns, Nicholas
Quarter-Final (1st leg)
Oct 8 vs Partick Thistle (a) 1-0
Att: 15,000 Nicholas (pen)
Quarter-Final (2nd leg)
Oct 20 vs Partick Th. (h) 2-1 (aet.) (agg. 3-1)
Att: 12,000 Burns, MacDonald
Semi-Final (1st leg)
Nov 12 vs Dundee United (a) 1-1
Att: 14,000 Nicholas
Semi-Final (2nd leg)
Nov 19 vs Dundee United (h) 0-3 (agg. 1-4)
Att: 21,000

1981/82 SEASON
Preliminary Round, Game One
Aug 8 vs St. Mirren (h) 1-3
Att: 26,100 McGarvey
Preliminary Round, Game Two
Aug 12 vs St. Johnstone (a) 0-2
Att: 10,406
Preliminary Round, Game Three
Aug 15 vs Hibernian (h) 4-1
Att: 19,200 MacLeod 2, Nicholas 2
Preliminary Round, Game Four
Aug 19 vs St. Johnstone (h) 4-1
Att: 14,600 Provan 2, McGarvey, Nicholas
Preliminary Round, Game Five
Aug 22 vs St. Mirren (a) 5-1
Att: 18,065 McCluskey 3, MacLeod 2
Preliminary Round, Game Six
Aug 26 vs Hibernian (a) 4-1
Att: 13,685 McGarvey 2, Sullivan, MacLeod

1982/83 SEASON
Preliminary Round, Game One
Aug 14 vs Dunfermline Athletic (h) 6-0
Att: McCluskey 2, Provan 2, McGarvey, Reid (pen)
Preliminary Round, Game Two
Aug 18 vs Alloa Athletic (h) 5-0
Att: 4,373 McCluskey, McStay, Burns, McGrain, Reid (pen)
Preliminary Round, Game Three
Aug 21 vs Arbroath (a) 3-0
Att: 5,275 McCluskey, Nicholas, Crainie
Preliminary Round, Game Four
Aug 25 vs Alloa Athletic (h) 4-1
Att: 6,100 Nicholas, MacLeod, Aitken, Burns
Preliminary Round, Game Five
Aug 28 vs Dunfermline Athletic (a) 7-1
Att: 8,000 Nicholas 4 (1 pen), Burns, R. Dall (og), McCluskey
Preliminary Round, Game Six
Sep 1 vs Arbroath (h) 4-1
Att: 5,202 Nicholas, McCluskey, Dobbin, MacLeod
Quarter-Final (1st leg)
Sep 8 vs Partick Thistle (h) 4-0
Att: 9,248 Provan, Nicholas, MacLeod, McGarvey
Quarter-Final (2nd leg)
Sep 22 vs Partick Thistle (a) 3-0 (agg. 7-0)
Att: 8,000 Nicholas 2, MacLeod
Semi-Final (1st leg)
Oct 27 vs Dundee United (h) 2-0
Att: 19,149 Nicholas (pen), McGarvey
Semi-Final (2nd leg)
Nov 10 vs Dundee United (a) 1-2 (agg. 3-2)
Att: 15,400 Nicholas

FINAL (at Hampden Park)
Dec 4 vs Rangers 2-1
Att: 55,372 Nicholas, MacLeod

1983/84 SEASON
2nd Round (1st leg)
Aug 2 vs Brechin City (a) 1-0
Att: 3,000 Melrose
2nd Round (1st leg)
Aug 27 vs Brechin City (h) 0-0 (agg. 1-0)
Att: 8,502
3rd Round, Game One
Aug 31 vs Airdrieonians (a) 6-1
Att: 9,000 MacLeod (pen), Provan, P. McStay, McGarvey, Whittaker, McLauchlan (og)
3rd Round, Game Two
Sep 7 vs Hibernian (h) 5-1
Att: 11,046 Reid 2 (1 pen), Melrose, P. McStay, McGarvey
3rd Round, Game Three
Oct 5 vs Kilmarnock (h) 1-1
Att: 5,435 MacLeod (pen)
3rd Round, Game Four
Oct 26 vs Hibernian (a) 0-0
Att: 9,000
3rd Round, Game Five
Nov 9 vs Airdrieonians (h) 0-0
Att: 5,216
3rd Round, Game Six
Nov 30 vs Kilmarnock (a) 1-0
Att: 9,000 Melrose
Semi-Final (1st leg)
Feb 22 vs Aberdeen (a) 0-0
Att: 23,000
Semi-Final (2nd leg)
Mar 10 vs Aberdeen (h) 1-0 (aggregate 1-0)
Att: 41,169 Melrose
FINAL (at Hampden Park)
Mar 25 vs Rangers 2-3 (aet.) (90 mins. 2-2)
Att: 66,369 McClair, Reid (pen)

1984/85 SEASON
2nd Round
Aug 22 vs Dunfermline Athletic (a) 3-2
Att: 7,320 McClair 2, McInally
3rd Round
Aug 29 vs Airdrieonians (a) 4-0
Att: 11,411 Burns, McInally, Grant, McClair
Quarter-Final
Sep 4 vs Dundee United (a) 1-2 (aet.)
(90 minutes 1-1)
Att: 21,182 McInally

1985/86 SEASON
2nd Round
Aug 21 vs Queen of the South (a) 4-1
Att: 6,400 Johnston 2, McClair, McInally
3rd Round
Aug 28 vs Brechin City (h) 7-0
Att: 9,292 Johnston 2, Aitken (pen), McInally, Burns, McStay, Provan
Quarter-Final
Sep 4 vs Hibernian (a) 4-4 (aet.)
(90 minutes 3-3)
Att: 20,000 McClair 2 (1 pen), McGhee Hibernian won 4-3 on penalties

1986/87 SEASON
2nd Round
Aug 20 vs Airdrieonians (h) 2-0
Att: 15,000 McClair 2
3rd Round
Aug 28 vs Dumbarton (h) 3-0
Att: 11,300 Johnston 2, P. McStay
Quarter-Final
Sep 3 vs Aberdeen (a) 1-1 (aet.)
Att: 23,500 Johnston
Celtic won 4-2 on penalties

Semi-Final (at Hampden Park)
Sep 23 vs Motherwell 2-2 (aet.)
Att: 26,541 McClair, Aitken
Celtic won 5-4 on penalties
FINAL (at Hampden Park)
Oct 26 vs Rangers 1-2
Att: 74,219 McClair

1987/88 SEASON
2nd Round
Aug 19 vs Forfar Athletic (h) 3-1
Att: 15,000 Walker 2, Stark
3rd Round
Aug 26 vs Dumbarton (a) 5-1
Att: 10,000 Stark 2, Burns, Walker, McGhee
Quarter-Final
Sep 1 vs Aberdeen (a) 0-1
Att: 24,000

1988/89 SEASON
2nd Round
Aug 19 vs Ayr United (h) 4-1
Att: 25,044 Walker 2, McAvennie, Burns
3rd Round
Aug 24 vs Hamilton Academical (h) 7-2
Att: 23,109 Walker 2, McAvennie 2, Stark, Burns, Archdeacon
Quarter-Final
Aug 31 vs Dundee United (h) 0-2
Att: 21,350

1989/90 SEASON
2nd Round
Aug 15 vs Dumbarton (a) 3-0
Att: 8,500 McStay, Dziekanowski, Burns
3rd Round
Aug 22 vs Queen of the South (h) 2-0
Att: 20,074 Grant, Dziekanowski
Quarter-Final
Aug 30 vs Hearts (a) 2-2 (aet.) (90 mins 1-1)
Att: 25,218 Dziekanowski, Walker
Celtic won 3-1 on penalties
Semi-Final (at Hampden Park)
Sep 20 vs Aberdeen 0-1
Att: 45,367

1990/91 SEASON
2nd Round
Aug 22 vs Ayr United (h) 4-0
Att: 21,462 Elliott 2, Dziekanowski 2
3rd Round
Aug 29 vs Hamilton Academical (a) 1-0
Att: 9,168 Dziekanowski
Quarter-Final
Sep 5 vs Queen of the South (h) 2-1
Att: 18,699 Dziekanowski, Miller
Semi-Final (at Hampden Park)
Sep 25 vs Dundee United 2-0
Att: 49,975 Creaney, McStay
FINAL (at Hampden Park)
Oct 28 vs Rangers 1-2 (aet.) (90 mins. 1-1)
Att: 62,281 Elliott

1991/92 SEASON
2nd Round
Aug 21 vs Greenock Morton (a) 4-2
Att: 9,518 Nicholas 2, Creaney 2
3rd Round
Aug 27 vs Raith Rovers (h) 3-1
Att: 21,081 Miller, Creaney, Fulton
Quarter-Final
Sep 3 vs Airdrieonians (a) 0-0 (aet.)
Att: 45,191 Airdrieonians won 4-2 on penalties

1992/93 SEASON
2nd Round
Aug 12 vs Stirling Albion (a) 3-0
Att: 7,630 Coyne, Creaney 2

3rd Round
Aug 19 vs Dundee (h) 1-0
Att: 30,849 Payton
Quarter-Final
Aug 26 vs Heart of Midlothian (a) 2-1
Att: 21,502 Payton, Creaney
Semi-Final (at Hampden Park)
Sep 23 vs Aberdeen 0-1
Att: 40,618

1993/94 SEASON
2nd Round
Aug 10 vs Stirling Albion (a) 2-0
Att: 8,533 McGinlay, McAvennie
3rd Round
Aug 25 vs Arbroath (a) 9-1
Att: 5,364 Nicholas, McGinlay, McAvennie 3, Payton 3, McNally
Quarter-Final
Aug 31 vs Airdrieonians (h) 1-0
Att: 25,738 McAvennie
Semi-Final (at Ibrox Stadium)
Sep 22 vs Rangers 0-1
Att: 47,420

1994/95 SEASON
2nd Round
Aug 16 vs Ayr United (h) 1-0
Att: 8,182 Grant
3rd Round
Aug 31 vs Dundee (a) 2-1
Att: 11,431 Collins, Walker
Quarter-Final
Sep 21 vs Dundee United (h) 1-0
Att: 28,859 Collins
Semi-Final (at Ibrox Stadium)
Oct 26 vs Aberdeen 1-0
Att: 44,000 O'Neil B
FINAL (at Ibrox Stadium)
Nov 27 vs Raith Rovers 2-2 (aet.)
Att: 45,384 Walker, Nicholas
Raith Rovers won 6-5 on penalties

EUROPEAN CUP

1970/71 SEASON
1st Round (1st leg)
Sep 16 vs KPV Kokkola (h) 9-0
Att: 41,000 Hood 3, Wilson 2, Hughes, McNeill, Johnstone, Davidson
1st Round (2nd leg)
Sep 30 vs KPV Kokkola (a) 5-0 (agg. 14-0)
Att: 3,900 Wallace 2, Callaghan, Davidson, Lennox
2nd Round (1st leg)
Oct 21 vs Waterford (a) 7-0
Att: 48,000 Wallace 3, Murdoch 2, Macari 2
2nd Round (2nd leg)
Nov 4 vs Waterford (h) 3-2 (agg. 10-2)
Att: 19,000 Hughes, Johnstone 2
Quarter-Final (1st leg)
Mar 10 vs Ajax (h) 0-3
Att: 65,000
Quarter-Final (2nd leg)
Mar 24 vs Ajax (a) 1-0 (aggregate 1-3)
Att: 83,000 Johnstone

1971/72 SEASON
1st Round (1st leg)
Sep 15 vs BK 1903 Copenhagen (a) 1-2
Att: 8,000 Macari
1st Round (2nd leg)
Sep 29 vs Copenhagen (h) 3-1 (agg. 4-3)
Att: 53,000 Wallace 2, Callaghan
2nd Round (1st leg)
Oct 20 vs Sliema Wanderers (h) 5-0
Att: 30,000 Gemmill, Macari 2, Hood, Brogan

2nd Round (2nd leg)
Nov 3 vs Sliema Wands. (a) 2-1 (agg. 7-1)
Att: 15,000 Hood, Lennox
Quarter-Final (1st leg)
Mar 8 vs Ujpest Dozsa (a) 2-1
Att: 31,000 Horvath (og), Macari
Quarter-Final (2nd leg)
Mar 22 vs Ujpest Dozsa (h) 1-1 (agg. 3-2)
Att: 75,000 Macari
Semi-Final (1st leg)
Apr 5 vs Inter Milan (a) 0-0
Att: 75,000
Semi-Final (2nd leg)
Apr 19 vs Inter Milan (h) 0-0 (aet) (agg 0-0)
Att: 75,000 Inter won 5-4 on Penalties

1972/73 SEASON
1st Round (1st leg)
Sep 13 vs Rosenberg (h) 2-1
Att: 30,000 Macari, Deans
1st Round (2nd leg)
Sep 27 vs Rosenberg (a) 3-1 (aggregate 5-2)
Att: 14,000 Macari, Hood, Dalglish
2nd Round (1st leg)
Oct 25 vs Ujpest Dozsa (h) 2-1
Att: 55,000 Dalglish 2
2nd Round (2nd leg)
Nov 8 vs Ujpest Dozsa (a) 0-3 (agg. 2-4)
Att: 20,000

1973/74 SEASON
1st Round (1st leg)
Sep 19 vs Turun Palloseura (a) 6-1
Att: 3,100 Callaghan 2, Hood, Johnstone, Connelly (pen), Deans
1st Round (2nd leg)
Oct 3 vs Turun Palloseura (h) 3-0 (agg. 9-1)
Att: 18,000 Deans, Johnstone 2
2nd Round (1st leg)
Oct 24 vs Vejle (h) 0-0
Att: 30,000
2nd Round (2nd leg)
Nov 6 vs Vejle (a) 1-0 (aggregate 1-0)
Att: 19,000 Lennox
Quarter-Final (1st leg)
Feb 27 vs Basle (a) 2-3
Att: 25,000 Wilson, Dalglish
Quarter-Final (2nd leg)
Mar 20 vs Basle (h) 4-2 (aet.) (agg. 6-5)
Att: 71,000 Dalglish, Deans, Callaghan, Murray
Semi-Final (1st leg)
Apr 10 vs Atletico Madrid (h) 0-0
Att: 70,000
Semi-Final (2nd leg)
Apr 24 vs Atletico Madrid (a) 0-2 (agg. 0-2)
Att: 64,000

1974/75 SEASON
1st Round (1st leg)
Sep 18 vs Olympiakos (h) 1-1
Att: 40,000 Wilson
1st Round (2nd leg)
Oct 2 vs Olympiakos (a) 0-2 (aggregate 1-3)
Att: 45,000

1977/78 SEASON
1st Round (1st leg)
Sep 14 vs Jeunesse D'Esch (h) 5-0
Att: 22,000 McDonald, Wilson, Craig 2, McLaughlin
1st Round (2nd leg)
Sep 28 vs Jeun. D'Esch (a) 6-1 (agg. 11-1)
Att: 4,000 Lennox 2, Edvaldsson 2, Glavin, Craig

2nd Round (1st leg)
Oct 19 vs SSW Innsbruck (h) 2-1
Att: 30,000 Craig, Burns

2nd Round (2nd leg)
Nov 2 vs SSW Innsbruck (a) 0-3 (agg. 2-3)
Att: 22,000

1979/80 SEASON
1st Round (1st leg)
Sep 19 vs Partizan Tirana (a) 0-1
Att: 25,000

1st Round (2nd leg)
Oct 10 vs Partizan Tirana (h) 4-1 (agg. 4-2)
Att: 51,000 McDonald, Aitken 2, Davidson

2nd Round (1st leg)
Oct 24 vs Dundalk (h) 3-2
Att: 33,000, McCluskey G, Burns

2nd Round (2nd leg)
Nov 7 vs Dundalk (a) 0-0 (aggregate 3-2)
Att: 16,300

Quarter-Final (1st leg)
Mar 5 vs Real Madrid (h) 2-0
Att: 67,000 McCluskey G, Doyle

Quarter-Final (2nd leg)
Mar 19 vs Real Madrid (a) 0-3 (agg. 2-3)
Att: 110,000

1981/82 SEASON
1st Round (1st leg)
Sep 16 vs Juventus (h) 1-0
Att: 60,017 MacLeod

1st Round (2nd leg)
Sep 30 vs Juventus (a) 0-2 (aggregate 1-2)
Att: 70,000

1982/83 SEASON
1st Round (1st leg)
Sep 15 vs Ajax (h) 2-2
Att: 56,299 Nicholas (pen), McGarvey

1st Round (2nd leg)
Sep 29 vs Ajax (a) 2-1 (aggregate 4-3)
Att: 65,000, Nicholas, McCluskey

2nd Round (1st leg)
Oct 20 vs Real Sociedad (a) 0-2
Att: 31,000

2nd Round (2nd leg)
Nov 3 vs Real Sociedad (h) 2-1 (agg. 2-3)
Att: 54,874 MacLeod 2

1986/87 SEASON
1st Round (1st leg)
Sep 17 vs Shamrock Rovers (a) 1-0
Att: 18,000 MacLeod

1st Round (2nd leg)
Oct 1 vs Shamrock Rovers (h) 2-0 (aggregate 3-0)
Att: 27,272 Johnston 2

2nd Round (1st leg)
Oct 22 vs Dynamo Kiev (h) 1-1
Att: 47,858 Johnston

2nd Round (2nd leg)
Nov 5 vs Dynamo Kiev (a) 1-3 (agg. 2-4)
Att: 100,000 McGhee

1988/89 SEASON
1st Round (1st leg)
Sep 7 vs Honved (a) 0-1
Att: 8,000

1st Round (2nd leg)
Oct 5 vs Honved (h) 4-0 (aggregate 4-1)
Att: 42,763 Stark, Walker, McAvennie, McGhee

2nd Round (1st leg)
Oct 26 vs Werder Bremen (h) 0-1
Att: 50,624

2nd Round (2nd leg)
Nov 9 vs Werder Bremen (a) 0-0 (agg. 0-1)
Att: 38,980

UEFA CUP
1976/77 SEASON
1st Round (1st leg)
Sep 15 vs Wisla Krakow (h) 2-2
Att: 30,000 McDonald, Dalglish

1st Round (2nd leg)
Sep 29 vs Wisla Krakow (a) 0-2 (agg. 2-4)
Att: 45,005

1983/84 SEASON
1st Round (1st leg)
Sep 14 vs Aarhus (h) 1-0
Att: 23,569 Aitken

1st Round (2nd leg)
Sep 28 vs Aarhus (a) 4-1 (aggregate 5-1)
Att: 14,500 MacLeod, McGarvey, Aitken, Provan

2nd Round (1st leg)
Oct 19 vs Sporting Lisbon (a) 0-2
Att: 57,500

2nd Round (2nd leg)
Nov 2 vs Sporting Lisbon (h) 5-0 (agg. 5-2)
Att: 39,183 Burns, McAdam, McClair, MacLeod, McGarvey

3rd Round (1st leg)
Nov 23 vs Nottingham Forest (a) 0-0
Att: 32,017

3rd Round (2nd leg)
Dec 7 vs Nottingham For. (h) 1-2 (agg. 1-2)
Att: 66,938 MacLeod

1987/88 SEASON
1st Round (1st leg)
Sep 15 vs Borussia Dortmund (h) 2-1
Att: 41,400 Walker, Whyte

1st Round (2nd leg)
Sep 29 vs Bor. Dortmund (a) 0-2 (agg. 2-3)
Att: 54,000

1991/92 SEASON
1st Round (1st leg)
Sep 18 vs Ekeren (h) 2-0
Att: 27,410 Nicholas 2 (1 pen)

1st Round (2nd leg)
Oct 1 vs Ekeren (a) 1-1 (aggregate 3-1)
Att: 7,500 Galloway

2nd Round (1st leg)
Oct 22 vs Neuchatel Xamax (a) 1-5
Att: 11,300 O'Neil

2nd Round (2nd leg)
Nov 6 v Neuchatel Xamax (h) 1-0 (agg. 2-5)
Att: 25,454 Miller

1992/93 SEASON
1st Round (1st leg)
Sep 15 vs Cologne (a) 0-2
Att: 15,000

1st Round (2nd leg)
Sep 30 vs Cologne (h) 3-0 (aggregate 3-2)
Att: 30,747 McStay, Creaney, Collins

2nd Round (1st leg)
Oct 20 vs Borussia Dortmund (a) 0-1
Att: 35,803

2nd Round (2nd leg)
Nov 3 vs Bor. Dortmund (h) 1-2 (agg. 1-3)
Att: 31,578 Creaney

1993/94 SEASON
1st Round (1st leg)
Sep 14 vs Young Boys (a) 0-0
Att: 7,300

1st Round (2nd leg)
Sep 29 vs Young Boys (h) 1-0 (aet.)
Att: 21,500 Baumann (og)

2nd Round (1st leg)
Oct 20 vs Sporting Lisbon (h) 1-0
Att: 31,321 Creaney

2nd Round (2nd leg)
Nov 3 vs Sporting Lisbon (a) 0-2 (agg. 1-2)
Att: 60,000

EUROPEAN CUP-WINNERS CUP
1975/76 SEASON
1st Round (1st leg)
Sep 16 vs Value Reykjavik (a) 2-0
Att: 9,000 Wilson, McDonald

1st Round (2nd leg)
Oct 1 vs Valur Reykjavik (h) 7-0 (agg. 9-0)
Att: 16,000 Edvaldsson, Dalglish, McCluskey P (pen), Hood 2, Deans, Callaghan

2nd Round (1st leg)
Oct 22 vs Boavista (a) 0-0
Att: 25,000

2nd Round (2nd leg)
Nov 5 vs Boavista (h) 3-1 (aggregate 3-1)
Att: 37,000 Dalglish, Edvaldsson, Deans

Quarter-Final (1st leg)
Mar 3 vs Sachsenring Zwickau (h) 1-1
Att: 46,000 Dalglish

Quarter-Final (2nd leg)
Mar 17 vs Sach. Zwickau (a) 0-1 (agg. 1-2)
Att: 40,000

1980/81 SEASON
Preliminary Round (1st leg)
Aug 16 vs Diosgyoer Miskolc (h) 6-0
Att: 28,000 McGarvey 3, McCluskey G 2, Sullivan

Preliminary Round (2nd leg)
Sep 3 vs Diosgy. Miskolc (a) 1-2 (agg. 7-2)
Att: 8,000 Nicholas

1st Round (1st leg)
Sep 17 vs Poli. Timosoara (h) 2-1
Att: 30,000 Nicholas 2

1st Round (2nd leg)
Oct 1 vs Poli. Timosoara (a) 0-1 (agg. 2-2)
Att: 50,000 Poli. Timosoara won on Away Goals

1984/85 SEASON
1st Round (1st leg)
Sep 19 vs La Gantoise (a) 0-1
Att: 22,500

1st Round (2nd leg)
Oct 3 vs La Gantoise (h) 3-0 (aggregate 3-1)
Att: 32,749 McGarvey 2, McStay P

2nd Round (1st leg)
Oct 24 vs Rapid Vienna (a) 1-3
Att: 12,000 McClair

2nd Round (2nd leg)
Nov 7 vs Rapid Vienna (h) 3-0
Att: 48,813 McClair, MacLeod, Burns
UEFA ordered the match to be replayed

Replay (at Old Trafford)
Dec 12 vs Rapid Vienna 0-1 (aggregate 1-4)
Att: 51,550

1985/86 SEASON
1st Round (1st leg)
Sep 18 vs Atletico Madrid (a) 1-1
Att: 60,000 Johnston

1st Round (2nd leg)
Oct 2 vs Atletico Madrid (h) 1-2 (agg. 2-3)
Match played behind closed doors.   Aitken

1989/90 SEASON
1st Round (1st leg)
Sep 12 vs Partizan Belgrade (a) 1-2
Att: 15,000 Galloway

1st Round (2nd leg)
Sep 27 vs Part. Belgrade (h) 5-4 (agg. 6-6)
Att: 49,500 Dziekanowski 4, Walkers
Partizan Belgrade won on Away Goals

1970-71 SEASON

FIRST DIVISION

Celtic	34	25	6	3	89	23	56
Aberdeen	34	24	6	4	68	18	54
St. Johnstone	34	19	6	9	59	44	44
Rangers	34	16	9	9	58	34	41
Dundee	34	14	10	10	53	45	38
Dundee United	34	14	8	12	53	54	36
Falkirk	34	13	9	12	46	53	35
Morton	34	13	8	13	44	44	34
Motherwell	34	13	8	13	43	47	34
Airdrieonians	34	13	8	13	60	65	34
Heart of Midlothian	34	13	7	14	41	40	33
Hibernian	34	10	10	14	47	53	30
Kilmarnock	34	10	8	16	43	67	28
Ayr United	34	9	8	17	37	54	26
Clyde	34	8	10	16	33	59	26
Dunfermline Athletic	34	6	11	17	44	56	23
St. Mirren	34	7	9	18	38	56	23
Cowdenbeath	34	7	3	24	33	77	17

1971-72 SEASON

FIRST DIVISION

Celtic	34	28	4	2	96	28	60
Aberdeen	34	21	8	5	80	26	50
Rangers	34	21	2	11	71	38	44
Hibernian	34	19	6	9	62	34	44
Dundee	34	14	13	7	59	38	41
Heart of Midlothian	34	13	13	8	53	49	39
Partick Thistle	34	12	10	12	53	54	34
St. Johnstone	34	12	8	14	52	58	32
Dundee United	34	12	7	15	55	70	31
Motherwell	34	11	7	16	49	69	29
Kilmarnock	34	11	6	17	49	64	28
Ayr United	34	9	10	15	40	58	28
Morton	34	10	7	17	46	52	27
Falkirk	34	10	7	17	44	60	27
Airdrieonians	34	7	12	15	44	76	26
East Fife	34	5	15	14	34	61	25
Clyde	34	7	10	17	33	66	24
Dunfermline Athletic	34	7	9	18	31	50	23

1972-73 SEASON

FIRST DIVISION

Celtic	34	26	5	3	93	28	57
Rangers	34	26	4	4	74	30	56
Hibernian	34	19	7	8	74	33	45
Aberdeen	34	16	11	7	61	34	43
Dundee	34	17	9	8	68	43	43
Ayr United	34	16	8	10	50	51	40
Dundee United	34	17	5	12	56	51	39
Motherwell	34	11	9	14	38	48	31
East Fife	34	11	8	15	46	54	30
Heart of Midlothian	34	12	6	16	39	50	30
St. Johnstone	34	10	9	15	52	67	29
Morton	34	10	8	16	47	53	28
Partick Thistle	34	10	8	16	40	53	28
Falkirk	34	7	12	15	38	56	26
Arbroath	34	9	8	17	39	63	26
Dumbarton	34	6	11	17	43	72	23
Kilmarnock	34	7	8	19	40	71	22
Airdrieonians	34	4	8	22	34	75	16

1973-74 SEASON

FIRST DIVISION

Celtic	34	23	7	4	82	27	53
Hibernian	34	20	9	5	75	42	49
Rangers	34	21	6	7	67	34	48
Aberdeen	34	13	16	5	46	26	42
Dundee	34	16	7	11	67	48	39
Heart of Midlothian	34	14	10	10	54	43	38
Ayr United	34	15	8	11	44	40	38
Dundee United	34	15	7	12	55	51	37
Motherwell	34	14	7	13	45	40	35
Dumbarton	34	11	7	16	43	58	29
Partick Thistle	34	9	10	15	33	46	28
St. Johnstone	34	9	10	15	41	60	28
Arbroath	34	10	7	17	52	69	27
Morton	34	8	10	16	37	49	26
Clyde	34	8	9	17	29	65	25
Dunfermline Athletic	34	8	8	18	43	65	24
East Fife	34	9	6	19	26	51	24
Falkirk	34	4	14	16	33	58	22

1974-75 SEASON

FIRST DIVISION

Rangers	34	25	6	3	86	33	56
Hibernian	34	20	9	5	69	37	49
Celtic	34	20	5	9	81	41	45
Dundee United	34	19	7	8	72	43	45
Aberdeen	34	16	9	9	66	43	41
Dundee	34	16	6	12	48	42	38
Ayr United	34	14	8	11	50	61	36
Heart of Midlothian	34	11	13	10	47	52	35
St. Johnstone	34	11	12	11	41	44	34
Motherwell	34	14	5	15	52	57	33
Airdrieonians	34	11	9	14	43	55	31
Kilmarnock	34	8	15	11	52	68	31
Partick Thistle	34	10	10	14	48	62	30
Dumbarton	34	7	10	17	44	55	24
Dunfermline Athletic	34	7	9	18	46	66	23
Clyde	34	6	10	18	40	63	22
Morton	34	6	10	18	31	62	22
Arbroath	34	5	7	22	34	66	17

1975-76 SEASON

PREMIER DIVISION

Rangers	36	23	8	5	59	24	54
Celtic	36	21	6	9	71	42	48
Hibernian	36	20	7	9	58	40	43
Motherwell	36	16	8	12	57	49	40
Heart of Midlothian	36	13	9	14	39	44	35
Ayr United	36	14	5	17	46	59	33
Aberdeen	36	11	10	15	49	50	32
Dundee United	36	12	8	16	46	48	32
Dundee	36	11	10	15	49	62	32
St. Johnstone	36	3	5	28	29	79	11

1976-77 SEASON

SECOND DIVISION

Celtic	36	23	9	4	79	39	55
Rangers	36	18	10	8	62	37	46
Aberdeen	36	16	11	9	56	42	43
Dundee United	36	16	9	11	54	45	41
Partick Thistle	36	11	13	12	40	44	35
Hibernian	36	8	18	10	34	35	34
Motherwell	36	10	12	14	57	60	32
Ayr United	36	11	8	17	44	68	30
Heart of Midlothian	36	7	13	16	49	66	27
Kilmarnock	36	4	9	23	32	71	17

1977-78 SEASON

PREMIER DIVISION

Rangers	36	24	7	5	76	39	55
Aberdeen	36	22	9	5	68	29	53
Dundee United	36	16	8	12	42	32	40
Hibernian	36	15	7	14	51	43	37
Celtic	36	15	6	15	63	54	36
Motherwell	36	13	7	16	45	52	33
Partick Thistle	36	14	5	17	52	64	33
St. Mirren	36	11	8	17	52	63	30
Ayr United	36	9	6	21	36	68	24
Clydebank	36	6	7	23	23	64	19

1978-79 SEASON

PREMIER DIVISION

Celtic	36	21	6	9	61	37	48
Rangers	36	18	9	9	52	35	45
Dundee United	36	18	8	10	56	37	44
Aberdeen	36	13	14	9	59	36	40
Hibernian	36	12	13	11	44	48	37
St. Mirren	36	15	6	15	45	41	36
Morton	36	12	12	12	52	53	36
Partick Thistle	36	13	8	15	42	39	34
Heart of Midlothian	36	8	7	21	49	71	23
Motherwell	36	5	7	24	33	86	17

1979-80 SEASON

PREMIER DIVISION

Aberdeen	36	19	10	7	68	36	48
Celtic	36	18	11	7	61	38	47
St. Mirren	36	15	12	9	56	49	42
Dundee United	36	12	13	11	43	30	37
Rangers	36	15	7	14	50	46	37
Morton	36	14	8	14	51	46	36
Partick Thistle	36	11	14	11	43	47	36
Kilmarnock	36	11	11	14	36	52	33
Dundee	36	10	6	20	47	73	26
Hibernian	36	6	6	24	29	67	18

1980-81 SEASON

PREMIER DIVISION

Celtic	36	26	4	6	84	37	56
Aberdeen	36	19	11	6	61	26	49
Rangers	36	16	12	8	60	32	44
St. Mirren	36	18	8	10	56	47	44
Dundee United	36	17	9	10	66	42	43
Partick Thistle	36	10	10	16	32	48	30
Airdrieonians	36	10	9	17	36	55	29
Morton	36	10	8	18	36	58	28
Kilmarnock	36	5	9	22	23	65	19
Heart of Midlothian	36	6	6	24	27	71	18

1981-82 SEASON

PREMIER DIVISION

Celtic	36	24	7	5	79	33	55
Aberdeen	36	23	7	6	71	29	53
Rangers	36	16	11	9	57	45	43
Dundee United	36	15	10	11	61	38	40
St. Mirren	36	14	9	13	49	52	37
Hibernian	36	11	14	11	48	40	36
Morton	36	9	12	15	31	54	30
Dundee	36	11	4	21	46	72	26
Partick Thistle	36	6	10	20	35	59	22
Airdrieonians	36	5	8	23	31	76	18

1982-83 SEASON

PREMIER DIVISION

Dundee United	36	24	8	4	90	35	56
Celtic	36	25	5	6	90	36	55
Aberdeen	36	25	5	6	76	24	55
Rangers	36	13	12	11	52	41	38
St. Mirren	36	11	12	13	47	51	34
Dundee	36	9	11	16	42	53	29
Hibernian	36	11	7	18	35	51	29
Motherwell	36	11	5	20	39	73	27
Morton	36	6	8	22	30	74	20
Kilmarnock	36	3	11	22	28	91	17

1983-84 SEASON

PREMIER DIVISION

Aberdeen	36	25	7	4	78	21	57
Celtic	36	21	8	7	80	41	50
Dundee United	36	18	11	7	67	39	47
Rangers	36	15	12	9	53	41	42
Heart of Midlothian	36	10	16	10	38	47	36
St. Mirren	36	9	14	13	55	59	32
Hibernian	36	12	7	17	45	55	31
Dundee	36	11	5	20	50	74	27
St. Johnstone	36	10	3	23	36	81	23
Motherwell	36	4	7	25	31	75	15

1984-85 SEASON

PREMIER DIVISION

Aberdeen	36	27	5	4	89	26	59
Celtic	36	22	8	6	77	30	52
Dundee United	36	20	7	9	67	33	47
Rangers	36	13	12	11	47	38	38
St. Mirren	36	17	4	15	51	56	38
Dundee	36	15	7	14	48	50	37
Heart of Midlothian	36	13	5	18	47	64	31
Hibernian	36	10	7	19	38	61	27
Dumbarton	36	6	7	23	29	64	19
Morton	36	5	2	29	29	100	12

1985-86 SEASON

PREMIER DIVISION

Celtic	36	20	10	6	67	38	50
Heart of Midlothian	36	20	10	6	59	33	50
Dundee United	36	18	11	7	59	31	47
Aberdeen	36	16	12	8	62	31	44
Rangers	36	13	9	14	53	45	35
Dundee	36	14	7	15	45	51	35
St. Mirren	36	13	5	18	42	63	31
Hibernian	36	11	6	19	49	63	28
Motherwell	36	7	6	23	33	66	20
Clydebank	36	6	8	22	29	77	20

1986-87 SEASON

PREMIER DIVISION

Rangers	44	31	7	6	85	23	69
Celtic	44	27	9	8	90	41	63
Dundee United	44	24	12	8	66	36	60
Aberdeen	44	21	16	7	63	29	58
Heart of Midlothian	44	21	14	9	64	43	56
Dundee	44	18	12	14	74	57	48
St. Mirren	44	12	12	20	36	51	36
Motherwell	44	11	12	21	43	64	34
Hibernian	44	10	13	21	44	70	33
Falkirk	44	8	10	26	31	70	26
Clydebank	44	6	12	26	35	93	24
Hamilton Acad.	44	6	9	29	39	93	21

1987-88 SEASON

PREMIER DIVISION

Celtic	44	30	10	4	78	24	70
Heart of Midlothian	44	23	16	5	74	32	62
Rangers	44	26	8	10	85	34	60
Aberdeen	44	20	17	7	55	26	57
Dundee United	44	15	15	14	51	50	45
Dundee	44	18	7	19	71	63	43
Hibernian	44	12	19	13	41	43	43
Motherwell	44	13	10	21	37	56	36
St. Mirren	44	10	15	19	41	64	35
Falkirk	44	11	11	22	42	74	33
Dunfermline Athletic	44	9	10	25	45	81	28
Morton	44	3	10	31	27	100	16

1988-89 SEASON

PREMIER DIVISION

Rangers	36	26	4	6	62	26	56
Aberdeen	36	18	14	4	51	25	50
Celtic	36	21	4	11	66	44	46
Dundee United	36	16	12	8	44	26	44
Hibernian	36	13	9	14	37	36	35
Heart of Midlothian	36	9	13	14	35	42	31
St. Mirren	36	11	7	18	39	55	29
Dundee	36	9	10	17	34	48	28
Motherwell	36	7	13	16	35	44	27
Hamilton Acad.	36	6	2	28	19	76	14

1989-90 SEASON

PREMIER DIVISION

Rangers	36	20	11	5	48	19	51
Aberdeen	36	17	10	9	56	33	44
Heart of Midlothian	36	16	12	8	54	35	44
Dundee United	36	11	13	12	36	39	35
Celtic	36	10	14	12	37	37	34
Motherwell	36	11	12	13	43	47	34
Hibernian	36	12	10	14	34	41	34
Dunfermline Athletic	36	11	8	17	37	50	30
St. Mirren	36	10	10	16	28	48	30
Dundee	36	5	14	17	41	65	24

1990-91 SEASON

PREMIER DIVISION

Rangers	36	24	7	5	62	23	55
Aberdeen	36	22	9	5	62	27	53
Celtic	36	17	7	12	52	38	41
Dundee United	36	17	7	12	41	29	41
Heart of Midlothian	36	14	7	15	48	55	35
Motherwell	36	12	9	15	51	50	33
St. Johnstone	36	11	9	16	41	54	31
Dunfermline Athletic	36	8	11	17	38	61	27
Hibernian	36	6	13	17	24	51	25
St. Mirren	36	5	9	22	28	59	19

1991-92 SEASON

PREMIER DIVISION

Rangers	44	33	6	5	101	31	72
Heart of Midlothian	44	27	9	8	60	37	63
Celtic	44	26	10	8	88	42	62
Dundee United	44	19	13	12	66	50	51
Hibernian	44	16	17	11	53	45	49
Aberdeen	44	17	14	13	55	42	48
Airdrieonians	44	13	10	21	50	70	36
St. Johnstone	44	13	10	21	52	73	36
Falkirk	44	12	11	21	54	73	35
Motherwell	44	10	14	20	43	61	34
St. Mirren	44	6	12	26	33	73	24
Dunfermline Athletic	44	4	10	30	22	80	18

1992-93 SEASON

PREMIER DIVISION

Rangers	44	33	7	4	97	35	73
Aberdeen	44	27	10	7	87	36	64
Celtic	44	24	12	8	68	41	60
Dundee United	44	19	9	16	56	49	47
Heart of Midlothian	44	15	14	15	46	51	44
St. Johnstone	44	10	19	15	51	66	39
Hibernian	44	12	13	19	54	64	37
Partick Thistle	44	12	12	20	50	71	36
Motherwell	44	12	12	20	46	61	36
Dundee	44	11	12	21	48	68	34
Falkirk	44	11	7	26	60	86	29
Airdrieonians	44	6	17	21	35	70	29

1994-95 SEASON

PREMIER DIVISION

Rangers	36	20	9	7	60	35	69
Motherwell	36	14	12	10	50	50	54
Hibernian	36	12	17	7	49	37	53
Celtic	36	11	18	7	39	33	51
Falkirk	36	12	12	12	48	47	48
Heart of Midlothian	36	12	7	17	44	51	43
Kilmarnock	36	11	10	15	40	48	43
Partick Thistle	36	10	13	13	40	50	43
Aberdeen	36	10	11	15	43	46	41
Dundee United	36	9	9	18	40	56	36

1993-94 SEASON

PREMIER DIVISION

Rangers	44	22	14	8	74	41	58
Aberdeen	44	17	21	6	58	36	55
Motherwell	44	20	14	10	58	43	54
Celtic	44	15	20	9	51	38	50
Hibernian	44	16	15	13	53	48	47
Dundee United	44	11	20	13	47	48	42
Heart of Midlothian	44	11	20	13	37	43	42
Kilmarnock	44	12	16	16	36	45	40
Partick Thistle	44	12	16	16	46	57	40
St. Johnstone	44	10	20	14	35	47	40
Raith Rovers	44	6	19	19	46	76	31
Dundee	44	8	13	23	42	57	29